Growing a Healthy and Faithful Congregation

REV. DR. LORENO R. FLEMMINGS

GROWING A HEALTHY AND FAITHFUL CONGREGATION

iUniverse books may be ordered through booksellers or by contacting:

iUniverse
1663 Liberty Drive
Bloomington, IN 47403
www.iuniverse.com
844-349-9409

ISBN: 978-1-6632-2363-0 (sc)
ISBN: 978-1-6632-2365-4 (hc)
ISBN: 978-1-6632-2364-7 (e)

Print information available on the last page.

iUniverse rev. date: 01/20/2023

Dedication

This book is dedicated to the inspiration and precious memories of my beloved mother, the late Eva Joyce Flemmings, the late Rev. Dr. Robert L. Johnson, and the countless former and present pastors that provided the writer for the last eleven years with encouragement, wisdom, prayers, and support in the publication of this book.

Acknowledgements

I celebrate with praise and thanksgiving to Almighty God for his grace, strength, and mercies extended throughout my journey of completing this project.

This Health and Faithfulness project would not have been undertaken without the support, encouragement, and participation of the members and officers of First Baptist Church and five ministry leaders and their churches: Father Bruce Montgomery (former Rector) St. Martin's Episcopal Church; Former Pastor, Jimmy Miller, St. Thomas A.M.E. Zion Church; Kay Hurd, layperson and Former Pastor Roberto Fois, Trinity United Church; Pastor Tim Wolf, New Horizon Christian Fellowship Church; Pastor Alicea Esteban, Fountain of Living Water Church and the members and officers of First Baptist Church.

I extend my deep appreciation to the three project advisors (Christopher Brennan, Quinta Goode, and Melane Bower) for their editorial comments, keen and thoughtful insights, relevant questions and helpful critiques and suggestions for the duration of the project. A special acknowledgement to Melane for our weekly meetings, discussions, and technical assistance to the overall completion of the project.

Special thanks to my project review committee (Rev. Dr. Clifford Johnson, Winston Boston, and members of Somerville Area Ministerial Association (SAMA) who journeyed with the ministry leader and provided their thoughts, ideas, and suggestions to the dialogue of congregational health and faithfulness?

Finally, I would like to express my gratitude to my wife, Dr. Jacqueline D. Flemmings, family, and colleagues whose love, prayers and encouragement provided the continued support to work toward completion of the project.

Church growth calls all of us into risky engagement. The church of the 21st century will require us to relearn and adapt in ways that will challenge the inherited ideas, forms and traditions that have been practiced throughout the years. Growing a healthy and faithful church will require leaders, as Dr. Flemmings states, who are able to re-think, re-engage and re-imagine a way forward in this changing world.

In his 1931 book regarding the missional life of the church, *The Word and the World,* Emil Brunner wrote, "the church exists by mission...where there is no mission, there is no Church; and where there is neither Church nor mission, there is no faith." The church and its leaders can no longer fail to challenge the status quo. Growing a healthy and faithful congregation will require leaders who are led by the Spirit to challenge the church to adapt to God's mission in a constantly changing community and world.

Dr. Flemmings' years of experience, valuable research, and in-depth assessment of factors of health and faithfulness will help guide and nurture leaders who find themselves yearning to be healthier and more faithful to growing a church and to the mission of the church of Jesus Christ.

Rev. Miriam Méndez
Executive Minister and Senior Regional Pastor
American Baptist Churches of New Jersey

Foreword

Growing a Healthy and Faithful Congregation, the title of this book, should be a high concern of every local church pastor. I commend my friend, Rev. Dr. Loreno Flemmings, who would much rather be known as "Pastor," for taking on such an important task of presenting to twenty-first century pastors the challenge of responding to the decline in church attendance and the sagging commitment of Christians in the Protestant church. Using contemporary data and his insights gained over decades of ministry, Pastor Flemmings brings to our attention in a very pastoral way the challenges of both church health and church faithfulness.

For a work like this to be of practical value, it must be couched in real-life situations, not abstract, global observations. Thus, *Growing a Healthy and Faithful Congregation* surveys the life of six churches located in Somerset County, New Jersey. While the geography of these churches is not diverse, the profile of them is quite diverse, ranging from conservative to more liberal denominational churches. Though their theologies and communities differ in some ways, they share the same challenges, as well as mutual respect for one another. Pastor Flemmings has assisted this ecclesial and clerical unity through his own pastoral bearing. All who know

Loreno know him to be a caring spiritual leader whose passion transcends his own ministry.

This book is not a point-for-point "how to do it" fix it manual or a success story that encourages emulating the author's ministry – God knows we have enough of those, and they never work. Rather, you will find here a profound alertness to the challenges pastors and churches face as well as attitudes and principles that will help most any church respond to the challenges of the day.

Becoming healthy and faithful may not be symbiotic. Some churches may be healthy, or at least appear that way, but be focused too narrowly and internally to be faithful to Christ's concern for all individuals and communities. Perhaps they are too earthly minded to be heavenly good. Other churches may seem to be faithful but lack the vibrancy of health that demands creativity and growth. Perhaps they are too heavenly minded to be earthly good. Bringing health and faithfulness together is the challenge. *Growing a Healthy and Faithful Congregation* points the way. As you ponder the insights of Loreno Flemmings, may your own health and faithfulness grow into the Christlikeness to which we are all called.

Rev. David E. Schroeder, Ed. D.
Chancellor, Pillar College

People of varied ages in society have developed an attitude that expresses a belief that there is little value in the Church. Unfortunately, this attitude has even taken root in organized religion and the faith community as a whole has been impacted. This has resulted in low Church attendance and a major reduction in those persons normally committed to the mission of the Church. This emphasis has caused the faith community to wrestle and seek ways of reversing this trend. Dr. Loreno Flemmings brings enlightenment to a massively complicated subject and provides the reader the opportunity to interpret the underlying causes in Church decline.

Dr. Flemmings has appropriately taken the time to review and document his conversations with several Churches of different denominations that are challenged by the decline in Church attendance. All of them, along with the wider community, are seeking answers and ways in which they can restart their Churches in a manner that they may declare themselves as healthy congregations. In responding, Dr. Flemmings takes a serious look at the biblical and theological understandings of what Church growth is. This is an approach that is most desirable, for the mission of the Church is different than that of other institutions. His analysis explores the present as well as future realities which are important for persons or organizations seriously seeking answers to these troubling times in the life of the church. Dr. Flemmings rightfully leads the reader to create a strategic plan which is designed to assist the congregation in taking action towards removing the blocks that hinder the progress in becoming a healthy congregation

This book is a much needed one, as it will assist any leader or faith community in establishing new visions and a strong sense of being. The Health and Wellness Project will be read and appreciated by faith leaders and congregations.

Rev. Dr. Clifford I. Johnson, Pastor
Shiloh Baptist Church, Wilmington Delaware

When my colleague Rev. Dr. Loreno R. Flemmings asked me to write this foreword for *Growing a Healthy and Faithful Congregation,* I thought—not now. I just didn't have time to read another book. But as a Christian minister with nearly 40 years of service, I also thought, this is a book on church leadership that I would love to read.

Further, as a psychologist who has worked with individuals and families in the context of church and community, I know the importance of healthy churches in the healing process. Now, as professor and president of a Christian seminary focused on educating people to think critically, act justly, and lead faithfully, I knew this was a forward I had to write. The world stands in need of just such a book. I am humbled to offer my thoughts and recommendations.

In this book, Pastor Flemmings discusses the church's need to "***rethink***, ***re-engage***, and ***reimagine***" so that it grows. These three moves are critically important for the church. Many churches are struggling to survive, let alone thrive. In this current American context, it is important for leaders of the Church to discuss what it means to grow, particularly in a healthy and faithful manner. In this vein, Flemmings does not disappoint. He provides a treatise full of suggestions and resources for pastoral leaders. Anyone engaged in advancing the work of Jesus the Christ will benefit from his guidance around grappling with the challenges facing the 21st-century church.

Through this publication Flemmings writes as an experienced senior pastor of five churches and brings a wealth of knowledge and experience from his work as a city planner, urban mission consultant, and church health assessment consultant. Who better to instruct us on ways to re-engage believers and non-believers in a struggle for the soul of America?

Weaving between spiritual and secular challenges, Reverend Flemmings provides a profile of ailing and flourishing congregations. Specifically, he analyzes the responses of five congregations around the issues of ministry context and demographic composition; worship style; ministries, programs, and activities; and leadership style and structure. Throughout his presentation, Flemmings summarizes the transition so their missions and ministries.

Flemmings also provides a cogent chapter on Biblical and theological foundations to apply to our understanding of church growth. These principles are critical when responding to the contextual and cultural challenges he describes. Yet, it is his forecasting of the church's future that offers the most promise for church reimagining. It is as if Reverend Flemmings has identified the root cause of the diminishing church–paralysis and inertia. Now he offers the antidote. First, he points out an indisputable truth: the world is changing. He concludes what some have known, and others have resisted, for ages—that the church, too, must change. Then he offers sage advice to direct you on the path of change. His clear, concise, and researched suggestions provide a winning playbook for church leaders.

Many church leaders are overwhelmed with worry about how to save their churches from the decline in membership and money. Flemmings provides a careful analysis of the problem and offers clear and concrete solutions. Implementing them will be easier after reviewing the experiences of the surveyed churches. Revitalizing and reimagining your ministry will happen only after you hold your ministry up to a similar light. Though Flemmings' small sample prevents generalization, his analysis is universally applicable.

With these thoughts, let me offer my gratitude to Rev. Dr. Loreno R. Flemmings for bringing pride to his alma mater and gifting the ecclesiastical world with this book on church thriving in this contemporary age. His analysis of church health offers a roadmap for rethinking, reengaging, and reimagining the 21st century church. I truly hope your church's ability to prosper is enhanced by your reading of this book.

In Joy and In Justice,

Micah L. McCreary, MDiv, PHD, LCP
President, New Brunswick Theological Seminary
John Henry Livingston Professor of Theology
General Synod Professor of Theology, Reformed Church in America
Former Co-Pastor, Spring Creek Baptist Church

*If you are rea*ding this book, then church growth is probably a concern of yours. Whether it be specific to your own church or the local church in general, you have most likely been affected by the many challenges presented in this study. If challenges excite you, then living in today's world is an exciting time.

Today, we have more churches than ever, yet there is a marked decline in local church membership and growth, due in part to the COVID-19 pandemic that brought the world to a standstill in the spring of 2020 and shuttered the doors of thousands of congregations around the globe in the ensuing months. But several other factors from this phenomenon are also evident: a recessive economy, the great divide caused by advancing technology, and the present competition of worldly stimuli that all of us, particularly our youth are exposed to. This has resulted in a contemporary tendency to lean toward *independence* rather than *interdependence* with our neighboring communities. The good news, however, is that these present-day challenges, the trials, and tribulations that Jesus pointed to in John 16:33 are merely tests, and as Jesus encouraged, "In this world you will have trouble. But take heart! I have overcome the world." This is cause for excitement.

The fact that Jesus is empowered by God and empowers us, indicates remedies are at our disposal, that we have an advantage in our struggles, and that we are already equipped to meet these challenges and tests face to face with an ensured victory at hand. If Christ is still relevant, and I believe He is and always will be, then so is His gospel. The question then becomes: how do we present the gospel in a way that is inviting, engaging, and effective? Because of the riches of His glory, the possibilities are limitless. This is truly exciting.

Excitement comes under two conditions: when one *begins* something new and when one is *promised* something new. Whether you are on the verge of building a new congregation, envisioning church growth, or serving as a liaison between your community and your church, this book will guide you along in your journey.

To be honest, I have vacillated between both excitement and frustration in my own journey of serving in rural, suburban, and urban congregations. The many experiences of joys, hardships, successes, failures, and disappointments have enabled me to understand why some churches grow spiritually, numerically, and financially, while other churches decline.

By now you may be wondering just how this whole health and faithfulness project even came into existence. In 2004, the American Baptist Churches of New Jersey (ABCNJ) applied for and received a Small Church/Small Community Renewal Grant from American Baptist Home Mission Societies (formerly known as American Baptist Churches-National Ministries) and the Frank E. Clark Charitable Trust to fund a project assessing the health and faithfulness of Baptist churches in New Jersey. Dr. Lee Spitzer, Executive Minister/Senior Regional Pastor of ABCNJ, designed a methodology for the project outline in his book *Endless*

Possibilities. This methodology involved creating church surveys of seven health factors (caring, worship, relationship with pastor, discipleship, unity, spiritual gifts, and future-faith) and seven faithfulness factors (evangelism, social action, global mission, new church planting, youth ministry, accessibility, and giving).

In 2005, I was called to serve as the first African American pastor of First Baptist Church in Somerville, New Jersey, a predominately White American congregation who has maintained a Baptist presence in the town since 1843. In the late nineteenth century and throughout much of the twentieth century, the church witnessed exponential growth in membership, stewardship, ministries, and community outreach. The church today, however, is confronted with difficult challenges and decisions related to an aging membership, a reduction in staff and an old historic structure that needs major capital improvements (repairs to the furnace, roof, and electrical system). To date, the membership has changed from a predominately white American membership to a predominately African American congregation, consisting of 85 percent African Americans, ten percent White Americans, three percent Asian Americans, and two percent Hispanic Americans. Moreover, 65 percent of the members are over the age of sixty-five, retired, relocated, or living in nursing homes due to health-related illnesses. First Baptist, like other mainline congregations in America, is experiencing decline at a critical juncture in its history.

In 2006, First Baptist Church, where I serve as pastor, participated in the second cohort of ABCNJ's Health and Faithfulness Initiative. First Baptist completed the Church Health and Faithfulness questionnaire and greatly benefited from the results and findings. The leadership as well as church membership reviewed the report and worked toward completing action steps necessary to implement a healthier and more faithful congregation regarding improved youth and family involvement, worship, stewardship, social action, and spiritual disciplines.

In 2019, a presentation was given at the Somerville Ministerial Association (SAMA) monthly meeting requesting the continued support and participation of clergy and their churches in the Growing a Healthy and Faithful Church Project. SAMA is an association of churches that exists for the purpose to provide information on topics such as housing, homelessness, mental health, and other related topics that are vital to the health and welfare of local churches and communities. The clergy who attended were presented with preliminary research findings about First Baptist as well as other local churches experiencing congregational decline due to aging membership, diminishing financial, physical, and human resources; and a lack of community outreach to those with no religious affiliation.

While many pastors and laypersons may recognize a need for congregational change today, they may not know how to undertake the changes needed to grow a healthy and faithful congregation. Thus, my primary purpose in this book is to examine the mission and ministry of mainline churches in Somerset County, New Jersey, including my own, First Baptist Church, and their efforts to grow healthy and faithful churches while reaching out to families, children, and youth in the community. Through survey results, this book will specifically examine health and faithfulness factors of both pastoral and lay leadership. The factors of Christian discipleship, worship, ethnic, and cultural diversity and community outreach within six congregations in New Jersey: Saint Martin Episcopal Church, Bridgewater, Saint Thomas A.M.E. Zion Church, Somerville, Trinity United Church, Warren, New Horizon Christian Fellowship, Hillsborough, Fountain of Living Water, Somerville, and First Baptist Church, Somerville.

Overview of the Chapters

Chapter One defines and explores the issues and concerns of congregational growth and decline in the local church today. The profiles of six congregations will be examined considering their historical, cultural, and social setting. We will explore the role and relationship of the churches' affiliations with their denominations for church leadership and ministry support.

Chapter Two examines the factors of congregational growth and decline from the perspective of each participating congregation and their implications for outreach to youth, families, and children in the community. Pastors and lay leaders who participated in this project will provide their own experiences and assessment of the factors that have impacted the church's growth and development.

Chapter Three reviews the biblical, theological, and cultural understandings of congregational growth and decline. In addition, a review of major writings will be presented on the Church Growth Movement and the rationale for exploring other models of church growth, especially the missional church model.

Chapter Four examines the factors of health and faithfulness, missional and traditional ministries, pastoral and lay leadership, Christian discipleship, worship, ethnic and cultural diversity, and community outreach of six local congregations' efforts to reach families, youth, and children in the community.

Chapter Five examines the new realities of the present as well as future realities confronting the local church of the twenty-first century. We will explore the six congregations' abilities to adapt to transition and change, as well as issues surrounding the intergenerational gap, technology and the digital divide, race, ethnicity, and gender, moral, and ethical issues.

Chapter Six outlines the steps in the strategic planning process for local churches engaged in missional church growth. These steps involve building a supportive team, conducting an annual assessment of ministries, programs, and activities, constructing an action plan to determine the mission and ministry goals for the future, and a timetable for implementation of the action strategies by the congregation.

Finally, **Chapter Seven** summarizes the major learnings, experiences, successes, failures, and future challenges of pastors and the six surveyed churches to assist other local congregations who has may be addressing similar problems, issues, and concerns related to congregational growth and decline.

Why is it so important that we discuss, or even care about, the health and faithfulness of our churches? I believe the answer can be found in the parable of the vine and the vinedresser as Christ tells it to his disciples in John 15:1-5: "I am the true vine, and my Father is the gardener. He cuts off every branch in me that bears no fruit, while every branch that does bear fruit, he prunes so that it will be even more fruitful. You are already clean because of the word I have spoken to you. Remain in me, as I also remain in you. No branch can bear fruit by itself; it must remain in the vine. Neither can you bear fruit unless you remain in me. I am the vine; you are the branches. If you remain in me and I in you, you will bear much fruit; apart from me you can do nothing."

In all the unknowns of the world we live in today, there is one thing we must remember: how interconnected we all truly are, in contrast to the worldview that often bears sharp emphasis on individualism. Our houses of worship, with varying faith doctrines, traditions, and religious practices, must come to understand how connected we are to one another through Christ as the true vine and the Father as the vinedresser. In the Old Testament, the image of the vine and vinedresser is commonly used as a metaphor for representing the people of Israel and God (see Psalm 80; Isaiah 5). In the New Testament, by calling himself "the vine," Jesus identifies himself with Israel. He reveals himself as the true Israel, the fulfillment of all that our God called Israel to be. God had delivered the people from Egyptian bondage, but the people failed to thrive and grow spiritually as the chosen people of God. Time after time, they wandered away from God in their disobedience as they worshiped the gods of other nations. They strayed from the path that God had placed them on. Jesus has come as the true vine to give all people the opportunity to grow in a healthy and faithful relationship with God, the way God always intended for the Israelites. The church of the New Testament, similar to churches today represents the New Israel of God, and the New Israel of God is defined not simply by ethnicity since it includes both Jews and Gentiles (Romans 11). Moreover, the branches of churches today *must bear fruit*. If they do not bear a spiritual crop to the glory of the Lord, God will cut those branches off, while those who do yield such a harvest are pruned so that they will bear even more (John 15:2).

So, if you accept the challenge of exploring greater church health and faithfulness, I encourage you to keep three powerful "R" words in mind along the way: ***re-think, re-engage,*** and ***re-imagine***. Why? They are action words that precisely describe the critical tasks the contemporary church must undertake if it is truly serious about not just bearing fruit but accomplishing Christ's Great Commission in the world – starting right where every congregation exists within its own community. Ready? Let the challenge begin.

1

The Changing Church: Growth and Decline

Traditional mainline congregations in the twenty-first century are experiencing major changes historically and culturally. In this post-modern world, the church is being challenged to reshape and reclaim its mission, vision, and ministry for spiritual, numerical, and financial growth. Congregations are confronting changing social and economic conditions, as well as changing demographics based on age, gender, and race. This also includes multi-ethnic and cultural diversity in neighborhoods and communities.

Although recent statistics vary on the exact number, it is believed that several churches close throughout the United States each year. Considering this sobering reality, a growing number of traditional mainline churches in America—including the six congregations examined in this book—have reached a critical place of rethinking, reshaping, and re-envisioning how to accomplish the Great Commission of Christ in the twenty-first century. However, let's first look at a few critical statistics regarding the overall state of Christianity in the United States today.

Christians in America

According to the 2019 study, "In U.S., Decline of Christianity Continues at Rapid Pace," conducted by the Pew Research Center, 43 percent of adults surveyed in 2018 and 2019 described themselves as Protestant Christians, down from 51 percent in 2009. The data particularly reveals a wide gap between the Silent Generation and Baby Boomers (the oldest Americans) and Millennials (the youngest Americans) in their levels of religious affiliation. In fact, more than eight-in-ten members of the Silent Generation (those born between 1928 and 1945) describe themselves as Christians (84%), as do three-quarters of Baby Boomers (76%), in comparison to just half of Millennials (49%) who describe themselves as Christians. Four-in-ten are religious "nones," or those with no religious affiliation at all, and one-in-ten Millennials identify with non-Christian faiths.

In conjunction with a lack of religious affiliation, statistics for church attendance among Americans are just as disheartening. According to the same survey results, rates of religious attendance are also on the decline. Over the past decade, the percentage of Americans who reported attending religious services at least once or twice a month dropped by seven percent, while the percentage of those who claimed to have attended religious services less often (if at all) has risen by the same degree. In 2009, regular worship attenders (those who attend religious services at least once or twice a month) outnumbered those who attend services only occasionally or not at all by a 52%-to-47% margin. Those figures today, however, reveal a declining trend that shows there are now more Americans who attend religious services a few times a year or less (54%) than those who claim to attend at least monthly (45%).

When it comes to the younger generation, only about one-third of Millennials say they attend religious services at least once or twice a month. Roughly two-thirds of Millennials (64%) attend worship services a few times a year or less often, including approximately (40%) who seldom or never go. In fact, there are as many Millennials who say they "never" attend religious services (22%) as there are those who reportedly attend at least once a week (22%).

Statistics surrounding the un-churched, that is, those who have never had an affiliation or identification with a church, among older Americans have also evolved significantly. In the 2011 report, "Barna Describes Religious Changes Among Busters, Boomers, and Elders Since 1991," the Barna Group describes changes in numerous religious variables, including church attendance, that occurred over a 20-year time span (1991-2011) among the three oldest generational segments of American population: Builders (aka Elders), Baby Boomers, and Baby Busters. The pre-Boomer segments, also known as the Builders or Elders, represent a combination of those born between 1927-1945 and pre-1927 (Seniors) and reported an increase in the unchurched population by eight percent, where three out of ten adults aged 66 or older (29%) were unchurched. Similarly, the Baby Busters, or those born between 1965 and 1983, also experienced an eight percent increase in the unchurched population (i.e., those who did not attend a church service in at least six months outside of special events such as funerals or weddings), for a total unchurched population of 39%. According to the report, however, the most significant change took place among the Baby Boomers, the post-World War II group comprising those born between 1946 and 1964. Barna survey statistics revealed that, during the 20-year time span of 1991-2011, the percentage of unchurched Boomers increased dramatically, up more than 18 points to 41%, representing the most unchurched generational segment of the U.S. population.[1] The trend has only continued in more recent years, as evidenced by a 2019 Gallup poll that revealed a steady decline in church attendance within the ranks of Traditionalists and Baby Boomers as well as those belonging to the younger generations of Millennials and Generation X over several three-year time periods:[2]

Table 1.1. Changes in Church Membership by Generation, Over Time

	1998-2000 %	2008-2010 %	2018-2020 %	Change since 1998-2000
Traditionalists (born before 1946)	77	73	66	-11
Baby Boomers (born 1946-1964)	67	63	58	-9
Generation X (born 1965-1980)	62	57	50	-12
Millennials (born 1981-1996)	n/a	51	36	n/a

An examination of all these statistics clearly reveals that Christianity is on the decline. Although there is no question that the world and U.S. society are changing, the real question is: how is the church changing to confront these challenges? Many local congregations in general, and mainline churches, are at a critical juncture, especially amid recent societal challenges such as the COVID-19 pandemic and racial injustice.

Assessing a congregation's health and faithfulness will entail the difference between a congregation's survival and death, and whether it simply survives or thrives in the future. When you go to the doctor for a physical check-up, the physician will check your vital signs to determine whether you're healthy. In a similar manner, we're conducting a spiritual check-up of the health and faithfulness, of six congregations that are representative of many congregations throughout the United States, and we'll learn more about those congregations in the following chapter.

What are the key indicators for growing a healthy and faithful congregation? To gauge those indicators in the undertaken surveys, participating congregations received two questionnaires: a health questionnaire and a faithfulness questionnaire. For the health questionnaire, church leaders were tasked with identifying, on a scale of 1 to 5, the importance of six factors within their congregations: 1) clarity of the church's mission and/or vision; 2) authentic worship; 3) pastoral and church leadership; 4) discipleship; 5) caring and loving fellowship; and 6) core values. For the faithfulness questionnaire, the congregations ranked the importance of six additional categories that included: 1) evangelism and missional outreach; 2) stewardship; 3) outward community focus; 4) cultural and racial diversity; 5) social advocacy and networking; and 6) missions (global, national, state, and local).

We will take a closer look at each of these questionnaires and the congregations' survey results in Chapter Four. If we were to consider the concept of church health and faithfulness on a broader scale, however, we would discover there are four general predictors that cut across theological, societal, and denominational boundaries. These elements: mission; vision; core values; and spiritual pastoral and lay leadership are essential and attainable for churches that desire to pursue a healthier and more faithful congregational life. We will take a closer look at those predictors now.

1. Clarity of Mission: A mission statement focuses on today and what an organization does to achieve it. A vision statement focuses on tomorrow and what an organization wants to ultimately become. Both are vital in directing goals. A mission is different from a vision in that it states the purpose of why the church or organization exists, and a vision is the result of the mission being accomplished or achieved sometime in the future. In the context of the church, the mission statement expresses its core belief system in answering the questions: Who are we and who do we serve as Christ's representatives in our communities and the world? The mission should include a statement about our biblical understanding of ministry (what is our purpose), a theological understanding of who calls us to serve (Christian discipleship), and a missional understanding of where we are called to serve (local communities and the world). For example, the mission statement of Saddleback Church in California, where famed pastor Rick Warren is senior pastor, is: "To bring people to Jesus and to membership in his family, develop them to Christ-like maturity, and equip them for their ministry in the church and their life mission in the world in order to magnify God's name."[3]

A congregational mission statement is a carefully defined, concise, and focused statement of what the congregation seeks to become to the community and for what it wishes to be known. It's a statement of why the church exists, what it values, and measurable objectives to accomplish its mission. The mission statement should incorporate answers to the following questions: What do we do? Whom do we serve? How do we serve them? All too often the mission becomes an obscure statement of the past and placed on the shelf to visit as needed; however, it's vital for congregations to intentionally keep the mission before the congregation in a continuous effort to move from the past to the present reality. The mission should use active, not passive, verbs and should be the guide for congregational life.

In addition, the mission should connect a congregation to the community context by establishing the congregation's sense of religious identity. In other words, relating this identity to the needs of those the congregation aims to serve. The mission should answer the question of who is to be served, what service is for those inside the congregation, and what service is offered to those in the wider community. To be effective, the mission must be owned by the congregation's membership, committees, and staff. There is a difference between a mission and a mission statement. Until the mission is made real through the development of goals and objectives, it is merely a statement on a piece of paper. To be a mission fully lived, it requires specific, measurable, attainable, relevant, and time-bound goals and objectives.

2. Vision: A vision statement seeks to accomplish the mission by portraying a clear and succinct description of what the church would look like sometime in the future. John Bryson states: "A vision statement is a 'clear and succinct description of what the organization or community should look like after it successfully implements and achieves its fullest potential.'" The well-known Microsoft Corporation's vision statement is to "empower every person and every organization on the planet to achieve more.[4] This vision statement provides the employees with an understanding of the future direction and focus of the organization and what Microsoft would like to achieve over time.

Unlike the mission statement that portrays the existing reality of the congregation, a vision is a dream of what the congregation wants to make of itself. The vision answers the following question: What do we want the congregation to look like in the future, in five or ten years? How do our overall efforts in ministry, activities, programming, and outreach align with the vision? The vision needs to be developed by both pastoral and lay members of the congregation. Once a vision is written and agreed upon, a congregation can move from the status quo toward a new reality. The vision can provide the congregation with new and creative ways of rethinking and reimagining the future congregation. A vision should be reviewed annually as a congregation grows and accepts new challenges. The congregation should be on guard against limiting the vision in scope to what it perceives as possible.

It's important for the leadership to adopt a long-term perspective of the untapped potential of the congregation. It also must be specific and concrete so that it can be known and worked toward.

Moreover, the vision statement is a shared vision by the collective individual thoughts and desires of the people. Peter Senge, author of *The Fifth Discipline: The Art and Practice of a Learning Organization*, writes: "When a group of people come to share a vision for an organization [a congregation], each person sees their own picture of the organization at its best. Each shares responsibility for the whole, not just for their piece."[5] Vision is what takes us beyond the broader dimensions of the congregation and helps us to envision how the ministries and activities of a congregation fit into the larger, overarching portrait for the future of the congregation.

3. Core Values: Discovering a church's core values will help the congregation understand the beliefs, principles, and practices that guide the organization to accomplish its mission, vision, and ministry. Core values are crucial to understanding the attitudes and behavior that guide a church in its planning and decision-making about its present and future. They also provide the foundation by which church leadership and membership perform their ministry and fulfill their calling in the world. These values underlie the church's ministry efforts, govern members' interactions with each other, and guide the strategies that will be used to fulfill the church's mission.[6]

Moreover, the core values describe the unique character and personality of a congregation. For example, one of the core values may be, "Our church is a culturally and racially diverse community." Another may be, "Our church believes in active lay involvement in social outreach to the community." Other examples of church core values are truth, fellowship, worship, compassion, unity, love, acceptance, fruitfulness, holiness, prayer, excellence, integrity, discipleship, and empowerment.

Core values represent the expectations and values that form the congregation's heart and the unity of oneness that holds people together. The values provide a framework within which every member of the organization can operate with responsible freedom. When individuals fully embrace the organization's shared values, they build trust, create community, and hold everyone mutually accountable. Christ taught the disciples the Great Commandment: "Love the Lord your God with all your heart and with all your soul and with all your strength and with all your mind,' and 'Love your neighbor as yourself" (Luke 10:27). The purpose of establishing a set of values is to create a pattern of behavior that builds a culture which supports the ministry, mission, and vision of the congregation.[7]

4. Pastoral and Lay Leadership: Congregations who are interested in growing a healthy and faithful congregation must equip and build a supportive and spirit-led, missional pastoral and lay leadership team. While considering church traditions, principles, and practices, the leadership team must guide the process of change—being led by the Spirit—to challenge the church to adapt to God's mission in a constantly changing community and world.

In his article, "The Leadership We Need—Negotiating Up, Not Down," Gil Rendle, Senior Consultant of the Alban Institute, says this about leadership for the future: "We would need to move outside of cultural norms to value the strange gifts our new leaders would bring. Those leaders would need to be exceptionally mature and able to stand outside of cultural norms, knowing that their gifts are valuable."[8]

More importantly, leaders are required to possess the Christian characteristics and requirements for leadership as outlined in 1 Timothy 3:1–7, Titus 1:6–9, and 1 Peter 5:2. These scriptural passages provide the church with the characteristics of elders who were equivalent to today's pastors. First Timothy 3:8–13 provides the character qualities for deacons. In 2 Peter 1:3–9, Peter lists qualities for all Christians. Acts 6:3–5 provides other qualities for early church leaders, and Galatians 5:22-23 presents the fruit of the Spirit that should characterize all leaders regardless of their level of responsibility.

Other important and necessary character qualities for spiritual leadership are found in 2 Timothy 2:2, such as competence, trustworthiness, and teachability. It cannot be overstated that teachability is vital for all leaders to have in their calling to Christian service. A lack of teachability among pastoral and lay leadership may result in church stagnation and decline. Leaders must be learners, and when they stop learning, they cease to be effective in their leadership roles.

In addition to the four indicators of congregational health and faithfulness, the writer describes six important factors for every congregation to consider. These factors include understanding historical, traditional, and cultural practices: ministry context, congregational identity, church programs and activities, worship style, structure and authority, and community demographics.

The word "ministry" derives from the Greek word *diakoneo,* meaning "to serve," or *douleuo,* meaning "to serve as a slave."[9] In the New Testament, the ministry is regarded as service to God and to other people in his name. Jesus Himself provided the pattern for Christian ministry, that is, he came not to receive service, but to give it (see Matthew 20:28; Mark 10:45; and John 13:1-17). In each of the five congregational profiles, there are seven areas of health and faithfulness that are critical to accomplishing the churches' missions and ministries:

1. Ministry Context
2. Congregational Identity
3. Church Programs, Ministries, and Activities
4. Worship, Liturgy, and Style
5. Congregational Structure and Authority
6. Community Demographics

1. **Ministry context** is defined as the church and community setting—local, state, national, and global—in which the membership seeks to live out its mission and ministry.[10] It's important for every congregation to be aware of the social and cultural settings of its physical and natural boundaries. The demographic information on population, as well as social characteristics of the church and community, will provide us with a contextual perspective of the potential challenges and limitations for congregational growth.

2. **Congregational Identity** is defined as the persistent set of beliefs, values, patterns, symbols, stories, and style

that distinguish a congregation.[11] One writer defines it as "a congregation's acknowledgment of the inheritance of beliefs and practices about the Christian faith and life, and the purpose of the church that it has by virtue of being a Christian church and standing in that particular historical stream." The church's identity is important because it provides the foundation for the traditions, beliefs, values, and policies that make the congregation unique from other congregations in accomplishing the work and ministry of Christ. Programs consist of those plans, activities, and ministries through which a congregation expresses its mission, both to itself and those in the community. They include the norms, beliefs, and values of a congregation and how financial resources and energies are working toward accomplishing the mission and ministry.

3. Christian Ministries, Programs, and Activities

The Christian ministries, programs, and activities of the congregation is defined as the "organizational structure, plans, and activities through which a congregation expresses its mission and ministry both to itself, its own members, and to those outside."[12] This includes an understanding of the norms, beliefs, and values of the congregation past and present, as well as a review of the human resources and energies of its membership in working toward accomplishing its mission and ministry. This area was particularly used to assess the surveyed congregations' effectiveness in addressing the needs of church membership and outreach to the youth, children, and families within the community.

4. **Worship, Liturgy, and Style**

Worship is defined as "the direct acknowledgement of God, His nature, attributes, ways and claims, whether by the outgoing of the heart in praise and thanksgiving or by deed done in such acknowledgment" (Expository dictionary of New Testament Words).[13] The psalmist best expressed this when he wrote, "As the deer pants for streams of water, so my soul pants for you, my God" (Psalm 42:1). Liturgy represents the forms, styles, and rituals used in Christian worship. There are, of course, different styles of worship based upon the faith traditions of the local congregation. I will provide a description of the surveyed congregations' worship styles, forms, and liturgies, and their impact on the spiritual growth of the membership, in the next chapter.

5. **Church Structure and Authority** involve the organizational process that the congregation uses to accomplish its programs, ministries, and activities for the membership and outreach to the community. It is the process by which things are accomplished in the church both formally and informally, including discerning lines of authority from boards, judicial bodies, or denominations. For example, the congregation's authority is grounded in tradition, church polity, a board, or denominational authority.

6. **Community Demographics** have many different uses for local churches. The more we know about the people in our communities, the more effectively local congregations can understand and address their needs. The demographic information provides each church with the make-up of both its membership and the community, helps each congregation identify community needs as well as gaps in its service, and assesses a church's capacity for outreach and ability to provide holistic ministries.

These four predictors, the elements of mission, vision, core values, and leadership, as well as the six additional factors listed above, were key in assessing the health and faithfulness of the congregations surveyed. But as already mentioned, they are features that can be used across the board to analyze the health and faithfulness of just about any church congregation, including your own. To help you in this assessment, you will find at the end of this and each subsequent chapter a series of "Questions for Reflection" that can be used to analyze the health and faithfulness of your own congregation thoughtfully and prayerfully. In the next chapter, we will seek to determine how effective the surveyed congregations are in clarity of their mission and vision statements, histories, beliefs, values, and church ministries, all while holding their own unique Christian heritage consisting of beliefs and practices from various traditions.

We will explore the question of whether each congregation's traditions and ministry practices are meeting the present social and economic realities confronting the church in the twenty-first century. We will take a closer look at the identity of each congregation's Christian heritage (liturgies, hymns, Bible studies, evangelism, ministries, and church histories). Also, we will examine the question of whether, considering their past faith traditions, it's possible for each congregation to rethink their identity and become more relevant in accomplishing Christ's mission and ministry in the church and community.

Questions for Reflection

1. Using the four predictors of health and faithfulness – mission, vision, core values, and leadership – begin to construct a similar analysis for your own congregation.

2. How do the six factors of ministry context, congregational identity, church ministries, worship, church structure, and community demographics also factor into your analysis?

2

Profiles of the Six Churches

In this chapter, we will address the growing and vital issue of congregational growth and decline of six congregations: St. Martin's Episcopal Church; St. Thomas A.M.E. Zion Church; Trinity United Church; New Horizon Christian Fellowship Church; First Baptist Church and Fountain of Living Water Church. Five pastors and one church representative completed a congregational profile that examined the following factors that have contributed to the growth and decline in their congregations, including:

- the ministry context and demographic composition of the congregation;
- the congregation's worship style;
- the congregation's ministries, programs, and activities; and
- the congregation's leadership style and structure.

It's important to note that, while located near each other in the Northeastern state of New Jersey, the congregations surveyed represent thousands of churches throughout the United States. All were selected because of the shared key elements of being Protestant congregations that are active in the lives of their communities. The congregations are similar in size (with the exception of St. Martin's Church that has a slightly larger membership than the other churches surveyed), and most importantly, they are all in a period of transition.

St. Martin's Episcopal Church

St. Martin's was established in 1895 and has an active membership of 404 members. The church is located in a suburban bedroom community in Bridgewater, New Jersey. Denominationally, the church is part of the Episcopal Church, although it is an autonomous member of the diocese.

The structure and governance of Saint Martin's includes the priest, also known as the rector, who is elected by the congregation to oversee and tend to the spiritual life of the members. In addition to the rector, the congregation elects' people who they can trust to work with the priest to make decisions about the building and grounds, finances, the budget, and other related items. Collectively, they are called the "vestry," and they handle the church business between annual meetings. There are seven paid, full-time staff persons including the rector, administrator of St. Martin's Day School, and a school business manager. Also, there are seven part-time positions including the parish administrator, the director of Christian education, a music director, and four teachers at the day school. Weekly church and community activities include St. Martin's Day School, adult church school, church school, an infant nursery, three youth groups, an adult Bible study, and the Christian Formation Class.

Twenty-nine percent of members are age 18 or under; 6% of members are between the ages of 19-24; 6% of members are between the ages of 25-34; 12% of members are between the ages of 35-44; 16% of members are between the ages of 55-64; and 13% of members are 65 and above. Most of the membership is 90% Euro-American, 5 percent Asian American; 2 percent Hispanic American; 1.5 percent African American; and 1.5 percent Middle Eastern.

The church's mission statement reads:

> We at St. Martin's as members of the body of Christ believe God is calling us to a closer relationship with Jesus, which empowers us:
>
> - To enter a lifelong process of growth, healing, and wholeness;
> - To experience worship that connects our liturgy to our lives and the world and connects people to people, and people to God; and
> - To live out our Baptismal vows as a vital Christian community that reaches out to the world with compassion.

St. Martin's primary goals for the next five years are:

- Make disciples of Christ;
- Reach out in creative ways to the unchurched;
- Expand our outreach ministries to reach the needs of residents in Somerset County; and
- Use the technology of our day to help us build community within, and to make connections with those on the outside that are in need of spiritual direction.

We will discuss congregational goals of all the churches surveyed as they relate to survey answers in a later chapter.

St. Thomas A.M.E. Zion Church

St. Thomas A.M.E. Zion Church was founded in 1851 and has an active membership of 85 members. The church is located in a suburban community in Somerville, New Jersey. In 2012, the street on which St. Thomas A.M.E. Church stands was renamed Paul Robeson Boulevard in honor of Robeson's contributions to the church and the larger community.

The membership of St. Thomas is 95% African American and 5 percent Euro-American. Thirteen percent of its members are ages 12 and under; 7% are ages 13-24 and under; 40% are aged 25-64; and 40% are ages 65 and older. The governing authority of the African Methodist Episcopal Zion denomination is provided by the Board of Bishops, General Officers and the Book of Discipline.

An Episcopal system of governance provides leadership by the Board of Bishops. Their responsibilities are divided by regions or geographical areas called an episcopal district. The General Officers are the elected administrative department heads responsible to the denomination for providing the resources and services to unite the denomination.

St. Thomas is part of the Mid Atlantic I Episcopal District in the New Jersey Annual Conference. The Annual Conference is divided into two Districts which are supervised by presiding elders. The local church's leadership is the responsibility of the appointed pastor who organizes and serves the congregation.

Currently, there are two paid staff positions that consist of a full-time pastor and a part-time organist. The church property consists of a main sanctuary and fellowship hall. Weekly activities at St. Thomas consist of a Bible study, children and youth school, youth church, adult church school, and a women's ministry.

The vision of St. Thomas reads:

> A Church Growing Together, Equipped with Love to Serve.

The mission of St. Thomas reads:

> Faithfully Serving the Present Age to the Glory of God!

The goals statement of St. Thomas reads as follows:

Goal 1: Missions

- Intentionally assess the needs of our church members and community;
- Humbly reveal Christ by our service through acts of mercy by God's grace; and
- Respectfully engage in the interests of humanity by displaying the love of Christ.

Goal 2: Evangelism

- Fervently offer Christ by spreading the gospel through our lives and in our ministries;
- Passionately utilize our gifts and graces to reach, inspire, and encourage the lost; and
- Methodically expand our influence as instruments of God by being relevant and radical.

Goal 3: Christian Education

- Prayerfully as role models lead through educating and developing mature Christians;
- Strategically plan and develop programs that are practical, applicable, and rewarding; and
- Consistently promote the importance of learning the Scriptures and the things of God.

The hopes and dreams of the St. Thomas church for the next five years are:

1. Paying off the mortgage and debts;
2. Increasing congregational growth by welcoming people of all ethnic and cultural backgrounds; and
3. Obtaining a 501(c)(3) organizational status to develop programs and renovate and remodel present facilities.

Trinity United Church

Trinity United Church, located in the suburban community of Warren, New Jersey, was established in 1877 and has an active membership of 50 members. Administrative oversight of the church consists of nine elders and six committees. The church is affiliated denominationally with the Presbyterian Church of the United States of America (PCUSA) and the United Church of Christ (UCC).

Weekly church ministries and programs include children's church school, adult church school, and a weekly church program entitled "Godly Play." At the time of this writing, the church is without a pastor and is in the process of searching for one. The church staff consists of a part-time organist, a part-time secretary, and a part-time custodian.

There are no members under the age of 25; 15% are ages 25-44 and 85% are ages 45-64, with no members over the age of 65. Ninety percent of the members are Euro-American, six percent Asian American, and four percent African American.

The vision of Trinity United Church reads:

"Growing in Christ and Sharing in Love." Trinity affirms God's love, and welcomes people of every color, age, ethnicity, gender identity, sexual orientation, circumstance, and ability. The Spirit of Christ's love is recognized and celebrated in various ways through worship and Christian service within the community. The church's vision is "growing in faith and sharing in love."

The mission of Trinity United Church reads:

> To share in carrying on God's work of reconciliation in Warren and in the changing world, to serve the needs of all members and families of this congregation, the community, institutions, and nations, and to provide opportunities for men, women, and children to live creatively and become whole persons under the Lordship of Christ.

The following are Trinity's goals:

- To serve and honor all of God's children by sharing the love that Christ shares with us to people of every color, age, ethnicity, gender identity, sexual orientation, circumstance, and ability;
- To become good stewards of the gifts that God has given us, our environment, our minds, bodies, and spirits, and the talents and the treasures of this life;

- To grow in our faith and pass our beliefs to our children and all who wish to join us in our journey of faith; and
- To extend a loving welcome and provide all people the opportunity for full participation in the life and ministry of the church.

New Horizon Christian Fellowship Church

New Horizon Christian Fellowship Church was organized in 1990 and has an active membership of 60 members. The church conducts services at a local intermediate school in a suburban community in Hillsborough, New Jersey. Denominationally, New Horizon is affiliated with the Assemblies of God. New Horizon's vision is to glorify God by developing fully devoted followers of Jesus Christ to serve enthusiastically and magnetically attract others to Him.

The administrative overseer of New Horizon is the pastor, and he/she oversees the day-to-day affairs of the fellowship by delegating to the members and committees the responsibilities for Christian education, pastoral care, evangelism, and outreach. The composition of membership consists of 13 members ages 1-12; 9 members ages 13-18; 0 members ages 19-24; 17 members ages 25-34; 10 members ages 35-44; 5 members ages 45-54; 2 members ages 55-64; 2 members ages 65-79; and 2 members ages 80 or above.

The congregation has a contemporary worship style of service that is reflected in the spirit-filled praise, songs, prayers, and a mixture of drums, guitars, and a keyboard with one or more singers. Weekly educational activities include children's church school on Sunday mornings.

New Horizon Church is committed to fulfilling a four-fold mission:

- Evangelize the lost;
- Worship God;
- Disciple believers; and
- Show Compassion.

The goals of New Horizon for the next five years include:

- To grow in discipleship/spiritual maturity;
- Relocate to a permanent location that is owned by the church; and
- Engage the community in service projects.

First Baptist Church

First Baptist Church (FBC), where I currently serve as pastor, was organized in 1843, has an active membership of 75 members, and is affiliated with the American Baptist Churches, USA. Historically, the first meeting house was erected on Main Street in 1845. Later, as the membership continued to grow, a new structure was erected at its present location on the corner of High and Mercer Streets in Somerville, New Jersey. First Baptist was known as "The Baptist Church" because it was the only Baptist church in a predominantly Reformed Church community in Somerville.

First Baptist is a traditional mainline church and has for several years focused on evangelism, missions, and partnering with community service providers to address the social and physical needs of the marginalized in Somerville, New Jersey. At the time of this writing, most of its members are aging and, as a result, there is a sense of urgency for attracting families, youth, and children to the church.

The authority and governance of the church are solely held by the membership of the congregation, the pastor, board of deacons, and trustees (elected by the church at the annual business meeting), the appointment of members to serve on standing committees (Budget Committee, Christian Education Committee, and the Music Department, Missions, Preschool, Memorial, Flower, etc.), and perform the daily responsibilities of the church between annual meetings. The administrative staff consists of the pastor, a part-time church secretary, a preschool director, part-time teachers, and assistant teachers.

The vision of the church reads:

> To become Christ's disciples in the church, community, and the world in transforming lives for the kingdom of God.

In 2015 First Baptist revised its mission statement to the following:

> The Mission of First Baptist Church is to inspire and cultivate the presence of Christ through active ministries for all age groups of racial, cultural, and ethnic diversity in our neighborhood and community."

The goals of First Baptist are as follows:

- To outreach to families, youth, and children by providing ministries and activities that address their spiritual, social, and physical needs;
- To provide creative and dynamic Christian education and learning opportunities to help members grow spiritually in becoming disciples in Christ;
- To provide annual workshops, seminars, and retreats for church officers and members to better equip them for the work of the ministry; and
- To provide creative and alternative ways to partner with other Christian faith groups to develop traditional and blended worship with special services during the year.

The church membership is 1% ages 0-12; 0% ages 13-18; 2% ages 19-24; and 5% ages 25-34; 5% ages 35-44; 2% ages 45-54; 10% ages 55-64; 70% ages 65-79; and 5% ages 80 and above. The racial and ethnic makeup of the congregation is 85% Euro-American; 10% African American; three percent Asian American; and two percent Hispanic American.

Weekly church ministries and programs include adult church school, children's church school, First Baptist Preschool, adult Bible study, and the Middle Earth Somerville Youth Center, which provides a safe place and environment for at-risk youth in Somerville to engage in after-school homework assistance, counseling services, and recreational and mentoring activities. In May 2015, First Baptist Church established a lease agreement for an extended outreach ministry with the Fountain of Living Water (FLW) congregation, which is 100% Hispanic. FLWC has a congregation of 76 members in the following age ranges: 18 members ages 1-12; 10 members ages 13-18; 2 members ages 19-24; 3 members ages 25-34; 19 members ages 35-44; 9 members ages 45-54; 8 members ages 55-64; 5 members ages 65-79; and 2 members ages 80 and above.

Weekly ministries and program activities include worship services on Sunday afternoon, adult and youth Bible study on Tuesday evenings and alternate worship services for men, women, and youth on Thursday evenings. Other activities include the annual Vacation Bible School and special annual revival services for men, women, missions, and youth.

The Fountain of Living Water mission statement reads:

"To praise and glorify God through our Lord and Savior Jesus Christ who loves us and gave His life for us. We will teach and exalt all biblical teaching and evangelize to the community of Somerville, NJ."

The goals of Fountain of Living Water are as follows:

- To encourage and promote world evangelism;
- To approve and conduct all biblical teachings and to disapprove all anti-biblical teachings, conduct, and methods; and

- To promote a basis for fellowship among all Christians.

Ministry Context

Four of the six congregations in the study have served in their present physical location for several years: St. Martin, St. Thomas, Trinity United, and First Baptist, all of which are known for their rich history and stories about their Christian faith throughout the centuries. For example, St. Thomas is located across the street from the Somerville Middle School, and throughout the years has used the school auditorium to address community issues and concerns regarding education and health. First Baptist is known for its support of mission projects, both locally and overseas in Haiti (the building of a school for children), the Democratic Republic of Congo, and Russia in helping to provide school supplies, clothing, and food for children and their families. St. Martin is known for its outreach in establishing a preschool for students and families in Bridgewater, New Jersey. Trinity is known for its radical hospitality to persons of all races, gender, and ethnic backgrounds, and has opened its doors to and welcomed the lesbian, bisexual, gay, and transgender (LBGT) community as part of its congregation. New Horizon, a congregation that has utilized a local school's facilities to hold its worship services, seeks to reach out to younger families and children with a more contemporary style of worship, such as drums, guitars, and other related instruments.

Four clergy and one lay representative from each of the five congregations were asked to complete a congregational profile on their church and community's social and demographic characteristics. Four churches, St. Martin, St. Thomas, Trinity United, and New Horizon, indicated a significant percentage of youth, teenagers, and families that are an integral part of their congregations. It should be noted that, because Fountain of Living Water (FLWC) fell under the umbrella of First Baptist at the time the original surveys were conducted, they were not immediately asked to provide questionnaire data. Below is a table outlining each of the five churches by age group.

Churches in
Research Study Membership Percentages by Age Group

	0-12	13-18	19-24	25-44	45-64	65+
St. Martin's Episcopal	14%	15%	6%	19%	32%	13%
St. Thomas A.M.E. Zion	13%	7% (13-24)		40% (25-64)		40%
Trinity United	0%	0%	0%	15%	85%	0%
New Horizon Fellowship	22%	15%	0%	45%	12%	6%
First Baptist	1%	0%	2%	10%	12%	75%

First Baptist has a significant percentage of seniors and a low percentage of youth and families. Analysis of these membership demographics can help us understand how some congregations are growing while others are declining. This data information becomes critical for our churches to ask tough questions about visible signs that the church is on life support. How does bridging the cultural and generational differences provide an opportunity for our churches to grow spiritually? How can our current facilities be more conducive to attracting youth and families in more creative ways during the week, such as family movie nights and recreation?

Community Demographics

All five congregations are in Somerset County, New Jersey. St. Thomas and First Baptist are in Somerville; St. Martin in Bridgewater; New Horizon in Hillsborough; and Trinity United in Warren, New Jersey. The table below indicates the breakdown of communities by racial groups.

Somerset County, NJ 2020 Community Demographics[14]

Townships in Research Study	Percent of Township Population				
	African American	*Hispanic/ Latino*	*Euro-American*	*Asian-American*	*Total Population*
Somerville	14.0	28.7	58.3	14.5	12,588
Bridgewater	2.8	8.2	68.9	24.4	44,507
Hillsborough	5.3	9.1	71.9	17.8	40,454
Warren	1.8	6.3	73.1	22.3	15,961

Three of the congregations (St. Martin, Trinity, First Baptist and New Horizon) are in lower- to middle-class neighborhoods and have a majority White American membership. St. Thomas has a 99%, African American congregation, while just 10% of First Baptist's members are African American. St. Thomas is surrounded by a working-class neighborhood of low- to moderate-income residents. First Baptist, which is in proximity (less than a mile) to St. Thomas, is also surrounded by low- to moderate-income residents, some of whom are retired, some professionals, and some skilled laborers. Much of the church membership in both First Baptist and St. Thomas are from Somerville and the neighboring towns of Bridgewater and Bound Brook.

Congregational Identity

Four of the five churches would be considered mainline congregations based on their histories. **St. Martin** is known for its education, school, and community outreach through its various programs and ministries. Its pastor has a 35-year tenure and has established and maintained positive relationships with church staff, officers, members, and residents of the Bridgewater community.

For several years, **Trinity** has been instrumental in welcoming persons from the LBGT community as well as supporting community programs and projects that provide services to the homeless and poor. Trinity has an "Open and Affirming Statement" which reads:

> As we endeavor to live our vision, "Growing in Christ, Sharing in Love," we at Trinity United Church affirm that God's love, Christ's church, and the Spirit's power are for the people of every color, age, ethnicity, gender identity, sexual orientation, circumstance, and ability. Therefore, we extend a loving welcome, providing all people full participation in the life and ministry of the church. In the spirit of Christ's love, we recognize, celebrate, and give thanks for the diversity in which God has created us.

New Horizon is a contemporary church known for its various outreach activities in the community. The membership currently meets at a local high school and strives to be a visible beacon of light in addressing the social and economic issues in the Hillsborough community. The pastor coordinates an annual community event in recognition of the National Day of Prayer, which is instrumental in bringing faith communities together to offer prayer for the various groups.

St. Thomas' identity relates to the history of community activism that Paul Robeson was known for in addressing issues of justice, equality in education, and civil and voting rights. The church has sponsored educational forums, health seminars, and community revivals to call people back to restoration and a relationship with Christ.

First Baptist is known for its missions, both locally and globally. The church hosts the annual Christmas Care Jail Program that provides toys and related items to children of inmates that are incarcerated in the Somerset County jail.

In summary, the identities of the six congregations are directly related to their mission and vision statements, histories, beliefs, values, and church ministries. Each congregation holds its own unique Christian heritage consisting of beliefs and practices from their various traditions. Thus far, we have a deeper understanding of their Christian faith and how each church seeks to express itself in its congregational life, both internal and external. Later in our analysis, we'll explore the question of whether the congregation's traditions and ministry practices are meeting the present social and economic realities confronting the church in the twenty-first century. We will take a closer look at the identity of each congregation's Christian heritage: liturgies, hymns, Bible studies, evangelism, ministries, and church histories. Also, we will examine the question of whether, considering their past faith traditions, it is possible for each congregation to rethink their identity and become more relevant in accomplishing Christ's mission and ministry in the church and community for the 21st century.

Congregational Structure and Authority

The sixth area is the review of congregational structure and authority that provide the lines of authority, responsibility, and accountability for the work and ministry of the church. Four of the surveyed church's profiles have a hierarchical church structure that is accountable to its judiciary, general conference, and presbytery.

New Horizon is a member of the Assemblies of God government structure that represents a combination of congregational and Presbyterian principles. In this structure, the church is sovereign in the selection of pastor, owning and holding property, maintaining membership rolls, management of all local business and other activities, and its voluntary participation in denominational programs. District councils are formed to assist local churches (most following state boundaries) to accomplish Christ's mission and ministry. The district council conducts annual business meetings and has oversight of churches and ministers in their areas. Also, The General Presbytery serves as the second highest policy-making body for the church and serves as an advisory board for the Assemblies of God. The church's interests are cared for by a 20-member board of directors called the Executive Presbytery between the annual sessions. The General Council is the biennial business meeting of the U.S. Assemblies of God. The voting membership at the General Council consists of all licensed and ordained ministers and a lay delegate elected from each local church.

The General Convention is the governing body of the Episcopal Church for St. Martin's congregation. The Convention consists of a bicameral legislature that includes the House of Deputies and the House of Bishops, which is comprised of nearly 300 active and retired bishops. The Convention meets every three years and has the authority to amend the Constitution and Canons of the Episcopal Church; adopt a three-year church budget; authorize liturgical texts and amend the Book of Common Prayer; adopt communions and covenants with other churches; set qualifications for orders of ministry and office-holders; elect officers of the General Convention, the Executive Council, and members of boards; and delegate responsibilities to the committees, commissions, agencies, and boards of the Episcopal Church.

The Executive Council of the Episcopal Church is an elected body representing the entire church. In the three years between General Conventions, the Executive Council meets on a quarterly basis. The Executive Council also has the duty to carry out programs and policies adopted by the General Convention and to oversee the ministry and mission of the Episcopal Church. It should be noted that the Executive Council is comprised of 20 members elected by the General Convention (four bishops, four priests or deacons, and 12 lay leaders) and 18 members elected by Episcopal provinces.

The General Conference is the highest body of the African Methodist Episcopal Church for St. Thomas A.M.E. Zion and all other local churches. It consists of the bishops, as ex-officio presidents, and an equal number of ministerial and lay delegates, elected at the Annual Conferences and the Lay Electoral Colleges of the Annual Conferences. The General Conference meets quadrennially (every four years).

The Council of Bishops, which is the Executive Branch of the Connectional Church, has general oversight of the church during the interim of General Conferences. The Council meets annually at times and places designated by the majority of the Council and shall determine such other times, as may be deemed necessary, in the discharging of its responsibility as the Executive Branch of the African Methodist Episcopal Church. This Council holds at least two public sessions at each annual meeting. There are Presiding Elders who serve as mid-level managers and whom the bishops appoint to supervise the local churches in a Presiding Elder's District. The Presiding Elder meets with the local churches in the district at least once every three months for a Quarterly Conference, reports to the Bishop at the Annual Conference, and makes recommendations for pastoral appointments. It should be noted that pastors receive an annual appointment(charge) to a church based on the recommendation of the Presiding Elder and with the approval and final appointment of the bishop.

According to the United Church of Christ Constitution, "the basic unit of the life and organization of the United Church of Christ is the local church." Trinity United is considered a mixture of the congregational and Presbyterian form of governance. With the final authority on most church matters left in the hands of the local church, many view the United Church of Christ's government as being closer to congregationalism. However, pastoral oversight and ordination are conducted by Associations, and General Synod representation is given to Conferences instead of congregational delegates. The basic authority and structure of the United Church of Christ is the local church (also often called the congregation). Local churches have the freedom to govern themselves, establishing their own internal organizational structures and theological positions.

Thus, local church governance varies widely throughout the denomination. Some congregations, mainly of Congregational or Christian origin, have numerous relatively independent "boards" that oversee different aspects of church life, with annual or more frequent meetings (often conducted after worship service on a Sunday afternoon) of the entire congregation to elect officers, approve budgets, and set congregational policy.

First Baptist differs from the other churches in church organization or polity. The church polity for Baptist churches refers to its functions. This includes the policies that guide matters such as governance, decision-making, structure, and leadership. The difference is especially evident in how congregations of Christians are governed. One major difference between Baptists and many other religious denominations is that no person or group outside of a Baptist congregation is to have any authority over the church regarding beliefs, policies, and religious practices.

Moreover, all members within the church fellowship are part of the body of Christ and have equal voting rights and privileges in the governance of the church. In the Baptist church, Jesus is the Head of the Church, and the congregation, pastor, boards of deacons and trustees, and the various elected appointed officers, staff, and committees are responsible for the day-to-day decision-making of the church. Each member has the right to vote on church issues and concerns at the annual business meeting or special business meetings of the church. It should be noted that Baptist beliefs are not only compatible with polity but are also foundational for church polity. Therefore, for Baptists, the ultimate authority for a church rests not in the people but in Jesus Christ. Jesus is the head or Lord of the church (Ephesians 4:15; Philippians 2:11).

Church Programs, Ministries, and Activities

The church's programs, ministries, and activities focus on accomplishing Christ's mission and ministry. The profiles indicated a similarity among all surveyed churches in that the church's beliefs, religious practices, and policies are expressions lived out in the mission statements. There is also the commitment by the membership for leadership training, and allocation of financial, and physical resources to support programs, ministries, and activities.

Traditional congregations tend to be characterized as program-driven churches rather than mission-driven churches. The missional church is defined as "an authentic community of faith that primarily directs its ministry focus outward on the context in which it is located and the broader world beyond."[15] The church itself is a mission seeking to transform individuals, churches, communities, and the world for the kingdom of God.

Each of the surveyed churches has the following ministries: preaching; Christian education; worship; pastoral care and counseling; Bible study; evangelistic and outreach activities; missions; and women's, men's, youth's, and children's programs. First Baptist and St. Martin have a preschool and day school during the week, which provided academic and religious instruction to students. The majority of the churches' programs, ministries, and activities are inward rather than outward focused

Worship, Liturgy, and Style

A congregation's worship, liturgy, and style/form vary from traditional to less formal to contemporary (the definition of contemporary means "existing, occurring, or living at the same time: belonging to the same period of time)." The traditional worship service is characterized by churches that still adhere to the generally accepted formal liturgy based on its history, tradition, and religious and cultural identity.

According to the churches' profiles, three of them, St. Thomas A.M.E., St. Martin, and Trinity United fall into this category. These churches use denominational resources as the prescribed formal liturgy encompassing creeds, prayers, and responses for Sunday worship services. Their resources consist of the Book of Common Prayer, the Book of Discipline, and the Book of Worship. In addition, the lectionary is used to provide the scripture readings for the liturgical year and recommended prayers and music selections are provided as well.

First Baptist, like many other Baptist churches, has the flexibility to provide a worship liturgy based on the historical, cultural, and social dimensions of the congregation. The range can be formal, less formal, and/or praise and worship followed by scripture readings and the preached word by the pastor. The revised common lectionary is used by some Baptist churches for the scripture readings for the liturgical year.

New Horizon Christian Fellowship, however, has adopted a contemporary approach in its Sunday morning worship services. To worship in a style more appropriate and meaningful for people today rather than those who lived in past decades, the church uses a band with various instruments to worship and praise the Lord. Every generation will be confronted with the task of responding to the traditional and contemporary worship styles they feel most comfortable with, as well as those that address their needs and concerns. In this light, people of all ages will base their decisions on the use of projection screens versus hymnals, praise teams versus choirs, praise bands versus organ and piano, or the "feel" of the worship or the prescribed form of liturgy.

In all the surveyed churches, there is a clearly defined structure and authority that delineates the lines of responsibility of church leadership for accomplishing the work of the mission and ministry of Christ. Three of the churches, St. Thomas, St. Martin, and Trinity, work in cooperation with the diocese, district, and presbytery of their respective denominations. In the case of First Baptist and New Horizon, the administrative oversight and decision-making process of the church involves the pastor working cooperatively with staff and members of local boards and committees to accomplish the work of the church. The congregation holds the ultimate power and authority to make the final decisions on matters of importance. We will soon examine the decision-making processes by each of the congregations to determine their effectiveness or ineffectiveness in accomplishing the church's vision and mission.

The surveyed congregations vary in terms of their ministry context and activities, community demographics, and worship and leadership styles, but one thing is clear: they are all undoubtedly in a period of transition and social change. The question, as we will ultimately examine, is how these congregations can not only survive but thrive in the face of evolving transitions. Although there exists a consensus on the mission and ministry of the church as stated in Christ's Great Commission, there are different perspectives on how it can and should be accomplished.

In the next chapter, we will examine the historical, theological, and biblical foundations of church growth and decline. We will also review the missional growth literature and its influences on the local church in the 21st century. Finally, we will explore the relationship between church growth, church health, and church faithfulness among the surveyed churches.

Questions for Reflection

How would you compare your church to each of the profiled congregations? What are the key similarities and differences?

3

Historical, Biblical, and Theological Understandings of Church Growth

In this chapter, we will switch gears to discuss church growth. What exactly does it mean to "grow" the church? What does church growth look like? If you, as a church or ministry leader or a layperson, have ever considered those questions, you're certainly not alone. Before we continue our study of the surveyed churches, let's first look at the answers to those questions about church growth, from historical as well as biblical and theological standpoints. For our study of this important topic, we will examine five major church growth movements that have taken place in North America over the last half a century. Also, we will review the findings of several prominent theologians from these respective movements. While this review isn't comprehensive in scope, we will look closely enough at this topic to understand a few key elements.

Why should we study history and the findings of theologians from times past? In the early 1960s alone, most churches and major denominations in the United States experienced significant growth as well as a period of decline. This was enough to cause many church strategists, theorists, theologians, and church leaders of varying denominations to conduct research into the underlying issues of church decline. Because the resulting movements were instrumental in helping to restore and revitalize congregational vitality and growth in the United States, it would be beneficial for us to at least become familiar with the history surrounding them. Let's momentarily step back in time to understand the foundational history of the American church and its impact on congregational growth.

The Church Renewal Movement

The Church Renewal Movement was born in the 1960s and early 1970s out of a concerned response to the progressive decline in universal church membership, attendance, and an overall spiritual decline. "Church renewal," alternatively called "revival," "restoration," or "revitalization," was a term used among theologians and church leaders to represent the decline and desire for church revitalization, as well as both present and future renewal for effective ministry.

The response grew rapidly and resulted in numerous books being written on the subject, including *Body Life* by Ray Stedman (1972) and *The Taste of New Wine* by Keith Miller (1968). Many scholars and church leaders argued that for the local church to continue advancing its mission and fulfilling its vision, outdated church programs, and ministries that had once helped serve those purposes needed to be either revitalized or replaced. This was the case confronting many mainline churches during this period. Many had based their methods and strategies for effective ministry during the 1950s which were no longer serving the contemporary needs of their congregations and communities.

Church renewal theorist, Howard Snyder, held that the Church Growth Movement, in order to be effective, must be based on a biblical vision of the church as the vital community in the Kingdom of God. He writes:

> The Church's task is to live out its faith that Christ has in fact conquered the principalities and powers, and thus to work for the progressive manifestation of the Kingdom until Jesus Christ returns to earth finally and eternally the reign of God.[16]

God's plan through the Church and its mission is to "reconcile all things in Jesus Christ" (Eph.1:10; Col.1:17-20). Church growth is directly related to kingdom growth in that the Church is called to make disciples of peoples throughout the world, and this implies numeric growth. Snyder also believed that it is God's will not only to plant, evangelize, and grow the church, but also renew it. The importance of the exercise of spiritual gifts by members of the body of Christ is essential to the church's growth and renewal process.[17]

Over time, other sub-movements developed within the broader Church Renewal Movement. The *Ecumenical Approach* focused on changing existing church structures with an emphasis on social ministry based on deeds rather than words, while the *Laymen's Movement,* which was more conservative than the ecumenical approach, placed greater emphasis on the formation of small groups and prayer as key elements for spiritual growth. The Laymen's Movement eventually expanded nationwide and assisted in the development of retreat centers, group conferences, meditation, and seminars on the spiritual life. The *Yokefellow Movement,* led by Quaker philosopher and author D. Elton Trueblood, was similar to the Laymen's approach in placing emphasis on the daily practice of prayer, scripture reading, proportionate giving of money, and systematic Bible study, while a fourth sub-movement, the *Lay Witness Movement,* focused more on evangelistic efforts of spreading the gospel message of Jesus Christ.

While the Church Renewal Movement and its sub-movements were effective in their emphasis on social justice, small groups, Bible studies, and individual spiritual growth, it failed to offer a viable alternative approach to declining attendance, particularly among mainline churches and denominations. This provided an opportunity for mainline churches to address some of the social and economic issues of church growth in a post-modern world, although it also left the challenge of how to confront the changing demographics of urban communities.

The Pentecostal/Charismatic Movement

The Pentecostal/Charismatic Movement is considered an International Christian renewal movement. It continues to grow in popularity and, in fact, remains one of the fastest-growing forces within the Christian world today.[18] Historically, the movement traces its origins to 1906, at the Azusa Street Mission in Los Angeles, California, a Methodist-sponsored revival. At this revival, people claimed to have been "baptized by the Holy Spirit" in the manner recorded in Acts Chapter 2 during the celebration of Pentecost. People were also speaking in tongues and experienced healing miracles in a way that demonstrated a spiritual awakening and revival. Those who were present at the revival meetings responded to this spiritual awakening by evangelizing and sharing the gospel message with the lost across the United States, thus beginning the Pentecostal/Charismatic Movement.

The biblical foundation of the movement takes its name from the Greek words *charis,* which is the English transliteration of the Greek word for "grace," and *mata,* which is the Greek word meaning "gifts," Charismata, then, means "grace gifts," emphasizing the manifestations of the gifts and presence of the Holy Spirit.[19] These gifts are also known as the biblical "charisms," or spiritual gifts which purportedly give an individual influence or authority over large numbers of people. The prominent gifts among these "charisms" are speaking in tongues and prophesying. It is the strong belief among many Pentecostals and Charismatics that the manifestations of the Holy Spirit given to those in the first-century church are still experienced and practiced today.

New Horizon Christian Fellowship (NHCF) and Fountain of Living Water (FLW) congregations, two of the surveyed churches, are members of the Pentecostal/Charismatic movement. As members of this movement, the two congregations strongly believe in and practice the charismatic gifts mentioned by Paul in 1 Corinthians 12:4-11 (gifts of prophecy, speaking in tongues, miraculous healing). Pentecostals believe these spiritual gifts should be in full operation in the life of the Church, evidenced in the speaking in tongues (also known as *glossolalia*), laying on hands for divine healing, and prophecies as evidence of the Holy Spirit. Most Pentecostals' worship and prayer meetings consist of spirited singing, dancing, shouting "in the spirit," raising hands and arms in prayer, and oftentimes, anointing the sick with oil which is the primary reason for the movement's growth and popularity.

Today, the Pentecostal/Charismatic Movement is represented by denominations such as the Church of God in Christ, Assemblies of God, United Pentecostal Church, and the Pentecostal Holiness Church, just to name a few. However, the movement had its controversial elements, particularly the issue of theological interpretations surrounding the baptism of the Spirit. At the beginning of 20th century, the original Pentecostals hailed from a holiness background that identified the baptism of the Holy Spirit, and there were those Pentecostals who believed that speaking in tongues represented salvation at conversion and removal of the sinful nature from the believer. Other Pentecostals from the holiness denominations, however, rejected this interpretation of speaking in tongues as a work of grace. Throughout the 20th century, a movement of the Spirit spread throughout non-holiness denominations, while holiness denominations held firmly to their belief that speaking in tongues was among the gifts of the Spirit that ceased at the close of the formation of the New Testament. Consequently, there was a split in the movement and believers from the holiness churches formed their own Pentecostal denominations (the largest being the Assemblies of God), which did not identify the baptism of the Spirit with speaking in tongues. Evidence of the Pentecostal/Charismatic influence exists in many other denominations today such as Baptists, Episcopalians, and Lutherans, as well as non-denominational churches.

Church Growth Movement

The origins of the Church Growth Movement in North America can be traced to the movement's father, Donald A. McGavran, in 1955.[20] McGavran, a theologian, is most noted for his three core principles of church growth:

1. the realization that God wants the un-churched to be evangelized and become disciples and responsible members of the church;
2. discovering the causes of and decline of church growth is faithful ministry; and
3. churches should be encouraged to develop plans and strategies to evangelize people to Christ.[21]

McGavran's major work, *The Bridges of God,* and his later work, *Understanding Church Growth,* explain his core principles, particularly theological, ethical, missiological, and procedural procedures, in greater depth. According to McGavran, evangelism is not complete until the person is a responsible disciple of Christ – in other words, effective evangelism can be measured by numerical church growth. Second, once the person becomes a disciple of Christ, there is an ethical mandate to be accountable to make other disciples. His third, and perhaps most controversial principle, states that effective evangelism equates with disciples bringing other persons, families, and relatives of their own race, class, and culture to Christ. Finally, McGavran defines the main task of the Great Commission as bringing believers to a deeper commitment to Christ and active involvement in the church. The task of making disciples of believers is considered distinct and separate from the task of "teaching them to observe all things," which McGavran calls "perfecting."[22] His understanding of perfecting refers to the stage at which the whole community lives the Christian way of life.

The Church Growth Movement experienced four paradigm shifts: *Research Paradigm, Business Paradigm, Marketing Paradigm,* and the *Church Health Paradigm.*[23] The Research Paradigm occurred in the 1970s and focused on discovering facts about church growth and decline through research and uncovering social, economic, and religious data. As the Church Growth Movement grew, it sought to be responsive to the needs of local churches and pastors in North America from the resulting data it gathered.

The second shift, the *Business Paradigm,* took place in the 1980s and emphasized the need to assist pastors and local churches with strategic planning, goal setting, and evaluation of church programs and ministries. This business model became popular with the publication of the book, *Twelve Keys to an Effective Church* by Kennon L. Callahan (1983). In making the church more effective, Callahan recommended long-range planning to improve a church's financial resources, worship services, leadership, accessibility, parking, seating, objectives, and small groups. This model sought to place greater emphasis on improving the administrative and overall effectiveness of the church through organizational development.

A second shift occurred at the end of the 1980s by George Barna, who proposed a Marketing Paradigm for church growth. Bara's 1988 book, Marketing the Church, was instrumental in driving popular opinion regarding church growth in a new direction for the 1990s. In discovering the reason for the decline in church attendance, Barna made the case for the need for marketing techniques and tools to survey why or why not people failed to attend church and began employing marketing approaches to attract and win non-churched people to Christ. This extreme marketing emphasis, however, did not have the kind of impact that resulted in a significant increase in church attendance, and in some cases even turned people away.

The last major shift, the *Church Health Paradigm,* occurred in the 1990s and focused on church growth principles as they related to the health and well-being of the congregation. The church health approach became known with the publication of the books, *The Purpose Driven Church* by Rick Warren (1995), *Natural Church Development* by Christian Schwarz (1996), and *Becoming A. Healthy Church* by Stephen A. Macchia (1999). In this approach, the emphasis focused on assessing how well the church is working to fulfill its five purposes: worship, ministry, evangelism, fellowship, and discipleship.

Donald Hilliard, Jr., pastor, and writer defines church growth from a biblical model of health and faithfulness and argues that spiritual maturity among Christian believers represents both numerical and financial growth. He writes:

> True and healthy church growth is always initiated by God. It is a work of the Holy Spirit as the Lord Jesus exercises his headship over his body in order to form his people into his likeness.[24]

The key elements for Hilliard's biblical model of church growth can be found in the second chapter of the book of Acts (Acts 2:42-47), such as preaching and teaching, fellowship, prayer, ministry, compassion, unity, worship, and trust in God for the increase of the church. For Hilliard, the true measure of church growth is not in numbers, but in the spiritual maturity of the members of the body of Christ. When believers grow spiritually in their commitment to becoming followers of Christ, the church will experience spiritual growth as a congregation.

Emerging/Emergent Movement

By the late 1990s, the Emerging/Emergent Movement was emphasizing new conversations among youth leaders throughout the U.S. regarding a post-modern future of the church. Participants in this movement, also described as evangelical, post-evangelical, liberal, post-liberal, conservative, charismatic, neo charismatic, and post-charismatic, sought to live out their faith in what they perceived to be a post-modern society.

In contrast to the principle stating that the delivery method must change while the message never should, emerging leaders began declaring that the message, too, must also begin to change. The Emerging/Emergent Movement, which remained prevalent into the early 2000s, sought to engage participants in conversation and place emphasis on a wide range of different topics, with a common agreement among believers of the movement in their disillusionment with the organized and institutional church. Their primary focus, moreover, was on the transformation of Christian worship, evangelism, and the Christian community.

Theologically, the Emerging/Emergent Movement believed in the importance of: (1) identifying with the life of Jesus; (2) transforming the secular realm; and (3) living highly communal lives. Their primary church activities consisted of (1) welcoming the stranger; (2) serving with generosity; (3) participating as producers; (4) creating as created beings; (5) leading as a body; and (6) taking part in spiritual activities.

The Emerging/Emergent Movement focused primarily on ecumenism, as well as unity within the body of Christ among people with different religious and ethnic backgrounds and diversity within corporate worship. The movement derives its name from the idea that, as culture changes, there should be a response addressing the cultural shifts in society. In this light, the movement is categorized as post-modernist in its thinking.

The Missional Church Movement

The Missional Church Movement began in the late 1990s primarily through the work of Lesslie Newbigin, a missiologist and former missionary to India who had become concerned with the western world's deviation from Christianity. Throughout his experiences on the mission field, Newbigin later envisioned the western world as a mission field that needed to be won to Christ again.

The Missional Church Movement, which can be described as a church that is on a mission from God. The purpose of God's mission is twofold: to witness to God's loving nature through ministry (social action) and to witness to God's salvation work (evangelism). Other terms often used to describe missional include "sending" and "sent."[25] Since its inception, missional thinking has been developed by various groups, both liberal as well as conservative, and focuses on what it perceives as the *missio dei* (mission of God) in comparison to the *missio ecclesia* (mission of the church). In contrast to other movements, particularly the Church Growth Movement, the Missional Church Movement places equal emphasis on social action and evangelism as they relate to God's plan, while the Church Growth Movement was known to prioritize local evangelism efforts over social action.

Charles Van Engen, author of *God's Missionary People* (1991), presents a perspective based on the premise that church growth is rooted in a missiologically applied, evangelistically focused theory. He writes:

> For those in the Church to see themselves as the missionary people of God, they need to visualize the Christian community, as simultaneously a human organization and a divinely created organism. Its mission is both a gift and task, both spiritual and social.[26]

Van Engen's understanding is that the purpose of the church cannot be separated from the church's role in society. The church's nature, existence, and mission in the world are shaped by its missionary outreach to the un-churched in its ministry context, therefore, the priorities for the life of the church and ministry cannot focus only on the gathering and harvesting of people for discipleship. It should also include the social and cultural context of the church in reaching out to a changing community.

Craig Van Gelder, another major contributor to the missional movement, offers a perspective stemming from the belief that the Church Growth Movement lacks a sufficient understanding of church doctrine, which hinders it from being able to effectively engage the culture. For Van Gelder, understanding the nature of the church provides the foundation for understanding its mission and vision for developing and organizing its ministry for kingdom growth. He writes:

> It is the work of the Spirit that orchestrates the interaction between a congregation and the context in which it is located. The focus of the Spirit's ministry is always to lead the church into a redemptive ministry that seeks to transform both human behavior and organizational life as the church participates in God's mission in the world.[27]

Craig Van Gelder describes the church's mission mandate as threefold: nature, ministry, and organization.[28] God has created the *nature* of the church and its identity in relation to the world. *Ministry* is what the church does and what it is doing to accomplish Christ's mandate, therefore, the church's programs and activities flow out of the nature of the church and become part of the church's identity. The *organization* of the church addresses how the church organizes itself to accomplish its mission and ministry. Van Gelder states "that understanding the church as being missionary in nature represents a more holistic way of thinking about mission."[29]

Church history is a fascinating study, although we've only briefly touched on it here for the purposes of examining a broad definition of biblical church growth. During that examination, however, we can undeniably see that the missional church is, by its nature, created, equipped, and sent into the world by God to accomplish His mission and ministry. So, if that's true, one of the most urgent tasks of our mainline churches relates to their understanding of the mission according to the Great Commission – that is, how does the church, based on its historical and cultural heritage, reach out to people of varying racial, ethnic, social, and economic backgrounds in the community?

The Great Commission is accepted by most scholars as the church's mission and is located in other scriptures, including Mark 16:15, Luke 24:46-49, John 20:21, and Acts 1:8, but let's examine Matthew 28:18-20 specifically for its implications on church and missional growth:

> 18 Then Jesus came to them and said, "All authority in heaven and on earth has been given to me.
>
> 19 Therefore go and make disciples of all nations, baptizing them in the name of the Father and of the Son and of the Holy Spirit,
>
> 20 and teaching them to obey everything I have commanded you. And surely, I am with you always, to the very end of the age.

At the outset, it's important to point out that there is no mention of the Church in the Great Commission contained in these verses, however, Jesus' teaching ministry pointed in the direction of the future building and nurturing of a Christian community (Matthew 16:18). Although the primary audience of the Great Commission was originally the Jews, the text says, "all nations," which can be interpreted as both Jews and Gentiles (non-Jews) or peoples (equivalent to ethnic groups). This implies that a great challenge for the church today is to reach out to all peoples across racial, ethnic, and/or national boundaries.

Baptizing in the name of the Father, Son, and Holy Spirit represents the act of being placed into the reign of the triune God. The other major imperative is "teaching them to observe all things I have commanded you." The Christian ethic of "love thy neighbor as thyself" is at work in pointing to a holistic gospel that includes working on behalf of those in society who are suffering from social and economic injustice.[30] The commission ends with a promise to the disciples and those who would come after, "I am with you always, even until the end of the earth." This is Christ's promise of his continuing presence to be with the disciples to grow the church and the kingdom of God.

It can be arguably stated that the church has been weak in the area of making disciples and evangelizing people to be obedient to the Great Commission. As we've already seen from statistics discussed in an earlier chapter, there are more unbelievers of all age groups today than forty years ago. This points to a sense of urgency for our mainline churches to reclaim the Great Commission with the power and authority of Christ. Undoubtedly, the church needs to make disciples by baptizing and teaching them to observe God's truths as demonstrated in the life and ministry of Christ and to bring about personal and community transformation in the lives of people locally as well as throughout the world.

In his book *Strategic Disciple Making: A Practical Tool for Successful Ministry,* Aubrey Malphurs states that Jesus was succinct in his commission to the disciples and the church: "It wasn't just to teach or preach the Word, as important as that is. Nor was it evangelism alone, although this is emphasized as much as teaching. He expects his entire Church (not simply a few passionate disciple-makers) to move people along the continuum from pre-birth (unbelief) to the new birth (belief) and then to maturity (growth)."[31] As shown in table 2.2, the disciple-making continuum describes the process by which new believers grow and develop in their spiritual growth and development within the church to become agents of proclaiming, teaching, and making disciples of others in the kingdom of God. As new believers experience a new birth in Christ, they continue to grow in their understanding of God's word, mission, ministry, and service to others.[32]

Table 2.2. Disciple-making Continuum[33]

Non- Disciple	New Disciple	Growing Disciple
Pre-Birth (unbelief)	New Birth (belief)	Maturity (growth)

A greater emphasis on the teaching, understanding, and praxis of Christian discipleship needs to be instituted by Church leadership within the various church ministries, boards, and committees. With the local church's primary focus on discipleship, an opportunity is presented for new and existing members of the church to engage in a process of learning to become disciples that lead and reach others to have faith in Christ, as we see in Mark 1:16-17:

> As Jesus walked beside the Sea of Galilee, he saw Simon and his brother Andrew casting a net into the lake, for they were fishermen. "Come, follow me," Jesus said, "and I will send you out to fish for people."

From a missional perspective, spiritual growth is measured in terms of new believers growing in Christ and in relationship to one another as a member of the body of Christ. Hilliard argues "spiritual growth in a church may or may not lead to numerical and financial growth, but numerical and financial growth by themselves will never lead to spiritual growth."[34] While there is a general perception that increases in numbers and finances will enlarge the church's membership, apart from intentional spiritual growth and outreach to the community, the congregation will remain stagnant. Christian discipleship training must become the first priority for leadership and membership if the church is to be effective in reaching the unchurched in the community. To this end, as existing and new members are nurtured and trained to become committed disciples of Christ, they will be able to disciple others to become fishers of families, youth, and children in the community.

This leads us to additional factors of church growth, that is, theological beliefs and practices, and how they relate to the

Church's efforts to accomplish the Great Commission. Although the list is long and summarily includes beliefs regarding the Trinity, the Holy Spirit, salvation, eternal life, the Second Coming of Christ, the Kingdom of God, the Scriptures, Christian baptism, the Lord's Supper, and the Christian Sabbath, we will focus here primarily on three: the *theology* of the Church, the *kingdom of God,* and the *Trinity.*

The New Testament Church is defined in Greek as the *ekklesia,* or "a called-out people," denoting a company, or assembly of persons, called out, or selected and separated from a larger group. The word *ekklesia* is rendered "church" 110 times in the New Testament and refers to a visible, local congregation, or the company of disciples meeting at a given place and location.[35] In the New Testament, the term *ekklesia* refers to "a local congregation of Christian disciples meeting for worship and service."[36] Why is this important? From a Christian perspective, *ekklesia* has a two-fold significance: (1) it is used primarily to designate a visible, local congregation of Christian disciples, meeting for worship, instruction, and service; and (2) it is used in a secondary and figurative sense to denote the invisible company of believers on earth and in heaven.

The kingdom of God is defined by Van Gelder as "the redemptive reign of God and must serve as the foundation for defining the nature, ministry, and organization of the church."[37] He further points out that "the church must find its core identity in relation to God's redemptive reign as announced that the kingdom of God is near (Mark 1:14-15)."[38] In the Gospels, Jesus announced, to all persons hearing and responding to his words, to repent and believe the good news, that the kingdom of God was being manifest in the world, and that redemption was at hand. A central theme throughout Jesus' earthly ministry was the message of proclaiming the kingdom of God (Matthew 4:17; 4:23; 9:35; Mark 1:14-15). In Luke, Jesus says the purpose for which he was sent was to preach the kingdom of God. In Matthew, the kingdom is present, but not fully consummated (Matthew 3:2; 4:17; 10:7) and is revealed to the disciples by the work of the Holy Spirit (Matthew 12:28). This is particularly important because, as the kingdom of God, the church becomes God's agent in organizing its mission and ministry in and through the world by the work of the Spirit. Moreover, the church's nature, ministry, and organization are aligned with the reality, power, and intent of the kingdom of God.

To delve into our third factor, it can be said that the Trinity – Father, Son, and Holy Spirit are basic to our Christian faith. Lesslie Newbigin remarks on the theological perspective of the Trinity when he noted, "God sent His Son into the world to accomplish redemption, and the Father and the Son send the Spirit into the world to create the church and to lead it into participation in God's mission."[39] The church's mission is the proclamation of the kingdom of God, sharing the life of Christ, and doing the work of the Spirit in an intergenerational and multicultural society. For Newbigin, the church's mission isn't to a cause or program or activity, it is to Christ and the Christian community. In this regard, Dietrich Bonhoeffer contends:

> When God's Son took on flesh, he truly and bodily, out of pure grace, took on our being, our nature, ourselves. This was the eternal decree of the triune

> God. Now we are him. Wherever he is, he bears our flesh, he bears us. And where he is, there we are too... Christian community means community through and in Jesus Christ. Everything the Scriptures provide in the way of directions and rules for Christians' life together rests on this presupposition.[40]

What does this mean? Simply put, if the church is to build a Christian community that resembles the kingdom of God, it must be led by the Spirit to understand its identity, mission, and ministry as the instrument by which God is bringing about transformation in the lives of people, institutions, and structures for kingdom growth. Otherwise, the church will continue to be influenced by secularism and provide organized ministries and activities that are not focused on biblical and spiritual growth but rather on maintaining the church as an institution. Hilliard contends, "We who are faithful must discipline ourselves and sensitize our spirits to hear God's voice so that we may know the divine will and way. This is an indispensable prerequisite for healthy church growth."[41] The Spirit, therefore, should always be engaging the church to become more relevant and responsive to the changing social and cultural contexts within the wider community.

We've discussed quite a few points of consideration, from biblical and theological standpoints, regarding church growth in this chapter. The challenge, however, remains in front of us all, including the surveyed congregations to implement whatever is necessary for church growth. And now that we've defined church growth, the next question becomes, how do we bring about growth in a healthy and faithful manner? If you're still up for the challenge, let's now look at the factors that make a healthy, thriving, and faithful congregation.

Questions for Reflection

1. What is your own definition of "church growth"?

2. Do you agree or disagree with the theologians' biblical and theological thoughts as outlined in this chapter about what is necessary for church growth? What are your takeaways of how the biblical and theological understandings of church growth can be practiced in your local church?

4

Church Health and Faithfulness

Dear friend, I pray that you may enjoy good health and that all may go well with you, even as your soul is getting along well.—3 John 2

In this chapter, we'll explore the factors of church health and faithfulness and their implications for church growth. We'll begin by answering the question: How can mainline church leadership and membership learn from their church's history and present ministry context to reach out to community youth, families, and children in addressing cultural, social, and physical needs? In rethinking, refocusing, and reshaping their structures, missions, visions, and organizational structures, the surveyed congregations will be challenged to confront new realities and to create new forms of traditions, practices, and ministries designed to reach out to youth, families, and children from diverse ethnic, social, and racial backgrounds in constantly changing contexts.

In his book *Deep Change,* author Robert Quinn states that "organizations tend to lose focus on their mission and become stagnant over time. As this happens, they must make a conscious decision to change. If they do not, they will continue down the path of decline."[42] Quinn refers to this as the *deep change* or *slow death*. Considering the issue of *deep change,* it is imperative that the church leadership and membership of all five churches develop a missional church growth approach that will work toward outreach within the next three years. If not, these congregations may continue down the path of decline and *slow death,* and eventually cease to exist.

To grow church membership numerically, spiritually, and financially, it is also important to understand the life cycle of a congregation. Author Alice Mann describes the various stages of congregational growth and development in the fulfillment of the church's mission and ministry, as outlined in the Great Commission, by explaining that most churches go through a cycle of birth, formation, stability, decline, and death.[43] These stages take the form of a bell-shaped curve, as shown in Figure 1 below. Congregations identify their *birth* moments as "the earliest moments in history that members can recall significant or dramatic events that happened" that had a tremendous impact on the spiritual growth and development of the church.[44] For example, some of the older members of First Baptist recalled that, in the beginning, the church was simply called "The Baptist Church," as it was the only Baptist faith witness in Somerville in the 1800s. They also explained that it wasn't until the 1900s that other Baptist churches began forming in the area.

According to Mann, next is the *formation* stage, or the period of spiritual formation that provides the congregation with an understanding of its identity, vision, mission, worship, and its program and ministry contexts. In this stage, St. Thomas AME Zion developed and established its basic Christian foundation through teaching, worship, and community outreach to attract families, children, and youth to the church. During the 1950s and 1960s, the church had one adult choir, an active and growing Sunday school, annual Easter and Christmas plays and pageants, and was the central gathering location in the area for families on Friday evenings.

Presently, St. Thomas has seen its membership decline over the last twenty years. However, the church continues to reach out during the week, and on Fridays, to families through revivals for spiritual renewal, health and educational seminars and workshops, and social activities including roller skating, basketball, movies, and family games. Today, the church is finding new ways to engage in outreach ministry within the Somerville community.

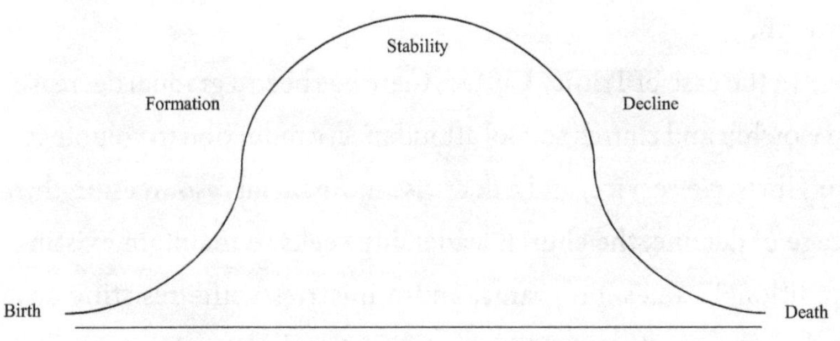

Figure 1. Life Cycle of a Congregation[45]

Mann describes the third stage at the top of the cycle as the period of *stability*. According to her, "stability is achieved when a congregation has forged a clear faith identity and has organized its life to express that faith effectively and persistently within its community context."[46] Here, the church has essentially plateaued and is now seeking to enjoy the benefits of their faithfulness and hard work in accomplishing the mission and ministry of Christ. For example, during the 1960s and mid-1970s, First Baptist experienced its greatest growth from 200 to 265 members. It had three choirs (adult, senior, and young adult choir) and a paid church staff which consisted of the pastor, secretary, pre-school director, organist, and a volunteer director of Christian education. This was a critical stage for First Baptist as well as similar churches that have peaked, because the tendency is to become stagnated and fail to reflect on where they are and how to plan for the future.

The fourth stage of Mann's cycle represents congregational *decline*. In this stage, the blame is shared amongst the pastor, church leadership, denomination, and community for the problems and issues confronting the church. Moreover, the members of the congregation fail to acknowledge the reality of stagnation of church growth.

In the case of Trinity United, there has been a gradual decrease in worship and church school attendance, a reduction in volunteers for Christian service, and a decrease in financial resources. In this stage of decline, the church leadership seeks to maintain existing traditional values, programs, and ministries while resisting any major changes that might cause conflict with the well-established members of the church. As a result, most of the decisions are made by a core group of long-tenured members serving in key leadership roles. These core members are operating with limited new and fresh ideas and lack the skills to attract families, children, and youth to the church.

Mann's final stage of the cycle is *death,* which occurs "if a congregation does not replace the blame response with a learning stance, or—if it waits too long—to try something new."[47] This stage is characterized by continued denial and blame, with limited attention and energy devoted to new lessons, ideas, and strategies in response to the changing ministry context in order to attract families, children, and youth to the church. As a result, as it confronts the reality of severely diminishing resources, the church's leadership and membership's primary focus is church maintenance and survival.

Mann describes another form of death as when "...a congregation dies because it has completed its task or because a changing environment is now calling forth a different kind of ministry."[48] Both factors are at work in not only the churches surveyed for this book, but also for many of the mainline churches today. There is a tendency by some churches to yearn for the return of "the good old days" of congregational growth, as they feel a sense of loss of church identity, purpose, and ministry context to attract families, children, and youth.

To avoid church decline that will eventually lead to death, churches must reclaim their vision, mission, program, context, and vibrancy so that they may work toward congregational change and community transformation. In one of the focus group sessions, pastors from the studied churches were asked to indicate where they felt their church was located on the life cycle of Alice Mann's diagram. Most indicated that their church was somewhere between decline and death. One pastor indicated that the church had once considered closing its doors – evidence that he felt his church, at that time, had been unable to sustain itself as a viable Christian witness in the community and was therefore confronting its own death.

So just what defines a healthy and faithful congregation? One definition of the word "health", as defined by the World Health Organization (WHO), is particularly useful: "Health is a state of complete physical, mental, and social well-being and not merely the absence of disease or infirmity."[49] Although this definition pertains to individuals and their mental, physical, emotional, social, and spiritual health, it can just as easily be applied to the church. This is especially true, because the church is made up of individuals whose overall health is the church's main concern. With this in mind, we can say a healthy and faithful congregation is "when church leaders and members strive to maintain their spiritual, physical, mental and social well-being and maturity for the purposes of growing the kingdom of God."

In the book of Acts, the church at Jerusalem is described as having the characteristics of a healthy and faithful church:

> They devoted themselves to the apostles' teaching and to fellowship, to the breaking of bread and to prayer. Everyone was filled with awe at the many wonders and signs performed by the apostles. All the believers were together and had everything

> in common. They sold property and possessions to give to anyone who had need. Every day they continued to meet together in the temple courts. They broke bread in their homes and ate together with glad and sincere hearts, praising God and enjoying the favor of all the people. And the Lord added to their number daily those who were being saved (Acts 2:42-47).

The four primary ministry areas of the early Church were the teaching and instruction of the apostles, the worship and fellowship among believers, regularly celebrating the Lord's ordinance of breaking bread, and praying together as a Christian faith community. They were diligent and consistent in receiving and accepting the apostles' teachings in the temple. They were a loving and caring Christian community, willing to sell their possessions and goods to help those most in need. They were together in unity of purpose and on one accord and had everything in common with one another. They continuously prayed together and offered thanksgiving of praise to God for all his miracles and wonders and for adding to the church of those being saved.

Church Health and Faithfulness Survey Results

I surveyed six pastors and one layperson of six congregations in Somerset County, New Jersey, all comprised of varying faith traditions, religious practices, and ministries. Each pastor received by e-mail a copy of the health and faithfulness surveys (Appendices

A and B), along with instructions on how to complete the survey and return to the writer upon completion. A summary of the data results for each congregation is listed below.

The results of the church health survey data indicated St. Martin's ranking as the highest among churches, while Trinity United scored the lowest in clarity of mission and vision. In the category of authentic worship, First Baptist and St. Martin's scored the highest while Trinity United scored the lowest. In the next category, New Horizon and St. Martin's scored the highest in providing effective pastoral and church leadership and Trinity United scored the lowest. In the category for discipleship, St. Martin's and New Horizon scored the highest, and Trinity United had the lowest score. St. Martin's and New Horizon also received the highest scores for congregational understanding and the practice of its core values, Trinity United scored average in this category with the need for improvement. It should be noted that, at the time of surveying the congregations, Trinity United was without a pastor and had just begun the search process for a new pastor.

The results of the faithfulness survey indicated First Baptist, St Martin's, and Trinity United scored the highest and New Horizon scored the lowest in evangelism. In the category of stewardship, St. Martin's, New Horizon, and Trinity United had the highest marks and First Baptist had the lowest. St. Martin's had the highest score and First Baptist had the lowest score in outreach to the community. First Baptist, St. Martin's, and Trinity United scored the highest and New Horizon scored the lowest in cultural and racial diversity. St. Martin's scored the highest and First Baptist, Trinity, and New Horizon scored the lowest in social advocacy and networking. First Baptist and New Horizon scored the highest and St Martin's and Trinity scored the lowest in missions.

Survey findings are summarized in the following line graphs, as well as a more detailed, individual analysis of each factor with a summary of key takeaway points.

Figure 1

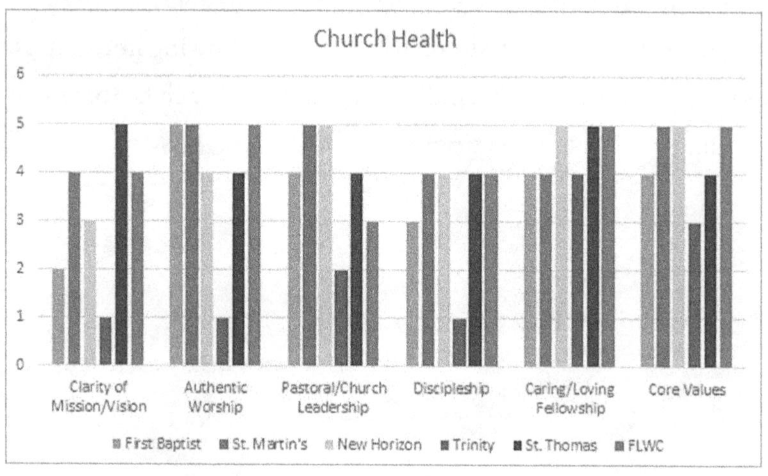

Key:

1 = Sense of urgency (members are greatly concerned and immediate attention is needed)

2 = Needs attention (we have concern and it needs attention)

3 = Good (we are average, nothing exceptional, and no real concern)

4 = Very good (we have made some progress)

5 = Exceptional (we have made great progress in working toward our mission and vision goals)

Figure 2

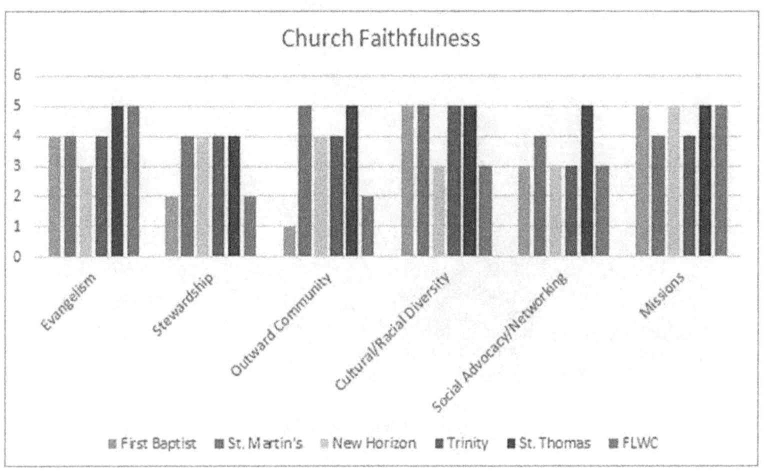

Key:

1 = Sense of urgency (members are greatly concerned and immediate attention is needed)
2 = Needs attention (we have concern and it needs attention)
3 = Good (we are average, nothing exceptional, and no real concern)
4 = Very good (we have made some progress)
5 = Exceptional (we have made great progress in working toward our mission and vision goals)

Figure 3

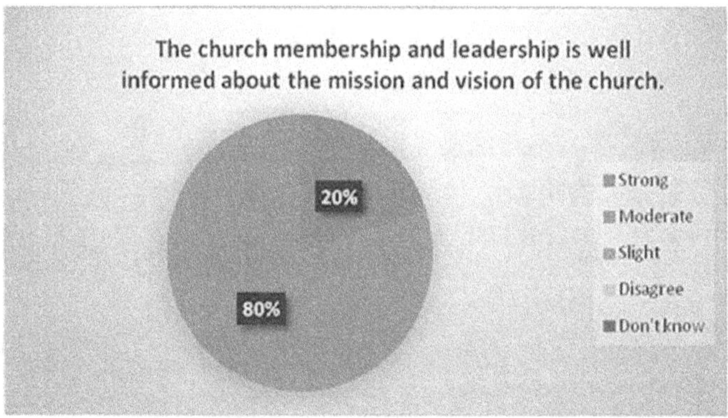

Mission and Vision

In response to the question as to whether church membership and leadership is informed about the mission and vision of the church, 80% of respondents indicated that they were moderately informed about the church's mission and vision. Approximately 20% of respondents felt strongly that they were well informed on the church's mission and vision. All respondents indicated a strong desire for the members to know the mission of the church.

- The development of a church's mission is important because it answers the questions of why the church exists, who it serves, and how it responds to the needs of the community.
- The vision of the church provides the membership with an understanding of where the church sees itself going or would like to be in the future.

Figure 4

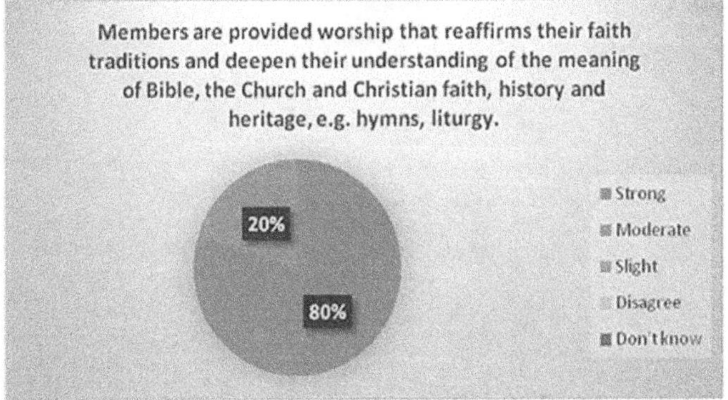

Authentic Worship

More than 80% of respondents strongly agreed and 20% of respondents moderately agreed that members are provided worship that reaffirms their faith traditions and deepens their understanding of the meaning of the Bible, the Church and Christian faith, history, and heritage.

- Churches that are intentional in their outreach to families, youth, and children must explore new ways of engaging the congregation in language, music, style, and various forms of relevant praise and worship.
- Worship must also address the spiritual needs of those whose lives are not shaped by the traditional and cultural values of baptized believers in Christ.

Figure 5

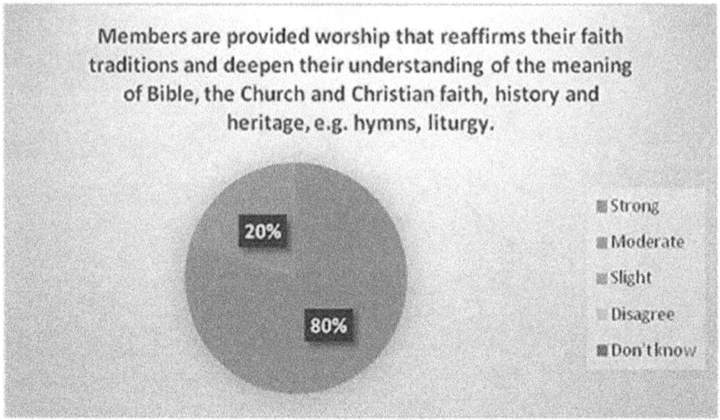

Pastoral & Lay Leadership

Survey findings indicated that 80% of respondents strongly agree that the pastor encouraged collaboration with laity to discover their spiritual gifts for ministry to the church and outreach to the community; 20% of respondents moderately agreed and felt the need to equip the laity for the work of ministry.

- Four decades ago, a major priority of accomplishing Christ's Commission of reaching out to others was an essential component of the ministry of many mainline churches; however, this does not seem to be a major emphasis today. Instead, most of a church's organized programs, ministries, and activities are concentrated on the inward growth of the church and not on the outward growth of inviting community families, youth, and children to church.
- Leadership must find the balance between traditional and existing religious practices, policies, and procedures

of the church by incorporating new, creative, and innovative programs and ministries that seek to address the unchurched and non-church population.

- It may also be necessary to replace the traditional, top-down leadership structure of most churches with a bottom-up leadership model that provides for empowerment of the laity to accomplish the mission and ministry of Christ.

Figure 6

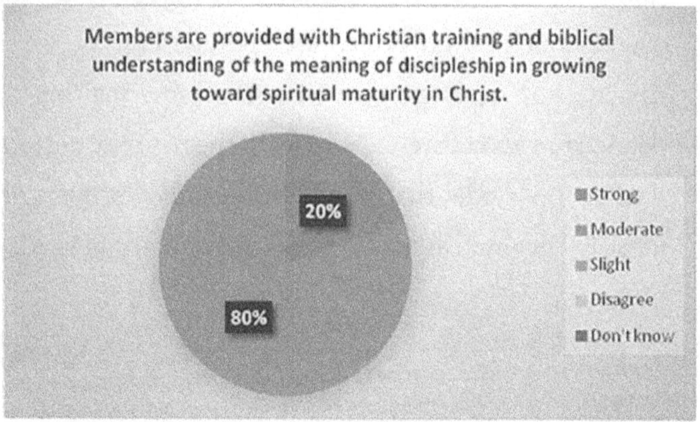

Discipleship

Survey findings indicated that 80% of respondents moderately agree that members are provided with Christian training and biblical understanding of discipleship in growing toward spiritual maturity in Christ. A percentage of 20% of respondents strongly agree that church members are trained in Christian discipleship.

- The word "disciple" means a learner, pupil, scholar, or one who comes to the taught. The idea of ***teaching*** and ***learning*** is crucial in this word.
- Christian discipleship is the process by which disciples grow and become equipped for service in the Lord Jesus Christ. Jesus Himself gave the command to make disciples (Matthew 4:19). In light of this verse's interpretation, every local church should have a discipleship training ministry for new and existing members to become fishers of people in winning others to Christ. However, pastors and lay

leadership are not always sure of what discipleship looks like or how to motivate and involve more people to make disciples.

- Stronger emphasis on the spiritual formation of Christian discipleship will help bring about a greater depth and appreciation of biblical and theological understanding of the church's mission and ministry.

Figure 7

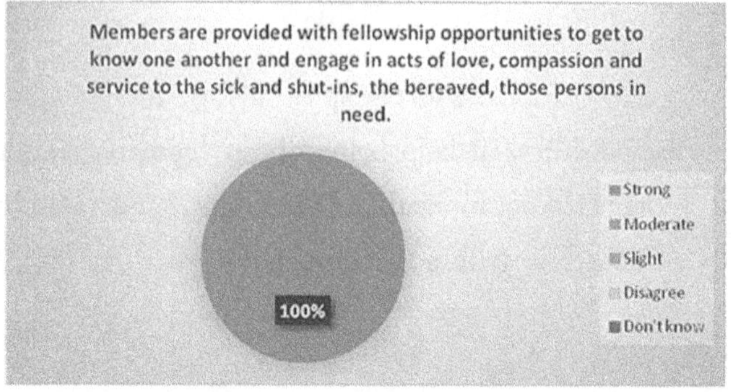

Caring & Loving Fellowship

Survey respondents unanimously agreed that their members are provided with fellowship opportunities to get to know one another and engage in acts of love, compassion, and service to the sick and shut-ins, bereaved and persons in need.

- There is a great need today for the church to address people with mental and physical disabilities and provide specialized ministries for members to become actively involved in the church.
- While many churches provide a caring and loving fellowship environment for members and first-time visitors, there are other forms of care and concern that needs to be extended for those who have become stigmatized in our society, including former prison inmates, alcohol and substance abusers, and individuals with HIV/AIDS and other related illnesses and diseases. However, the church becomes unhealthy when the pastor and a few members are the only ones showing care for others or when congregation members limit their care and concern only to those within the congregation.

Figure 8

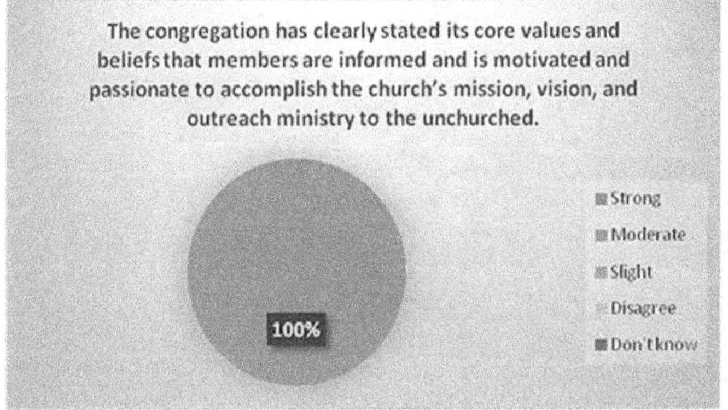

Core Values

When asked about core values, survey respondents were unanimous that their congregations had a moderate understanding of the core values and beliefs of the church, that members were informed concerning those core values and beliefs, and that they were motivated and passionate to accomplish the church's mission, vision, and outreach ministry to the community.

- It is crucial that a church's core values be embraced by both leadership and membership and implemented within the overall church programs, ministries, and activities on a daily basis. In doing so, the church will seek to live out the true meaning and purpose of its existence: building the kingdom of God on earth.
- There may exist a lack of understanding of the church's core values, which could result in members not being more actively involved in the church. For this reason, core values should be a matter of regular review for every congregation.

Figure 9

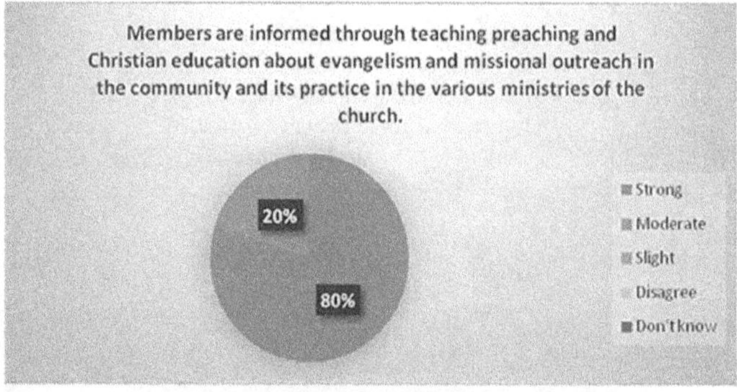

Evangelism & Missional Outreach

Survey results indicated that 80% of respondents indicated strongly that members are informed through teaching, preaching, and Christian education about evangelism and missional outreach in the community and its practice in the various ministries of the church; 20% of respondents indicated strongly that they are informed about evangelism and missional outreach but that it is not practiced regularly in the various ministries of the church.

- Most churches sense a responsibility to reach out to the world outside their walls, but they respond to this call in different ways. Some churches focus on the spiritual dimension of human need, helping people develop a relationship with God, while others emphasize people's social and emotional well-being by providing services or advocating for justice. Still, others attempt to blend these priorities.
- It is important for congregations that provide social services to the community to find ways to integrate sharing their faith while also meeting the social and economic needs of individuals.

Figure 10

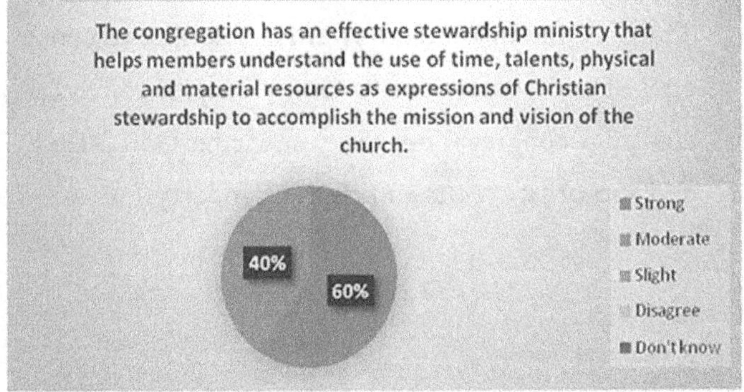

Stewardship

Survey findings indicated that 60% of participants surveyed indicated that the congregation is strong and has an effective stewardship ministry that helps members understand their use of time, talents, physical, and material resources as expressions of Christian stewardship to accomplish the mission and ministry of the church. This was followed by 40% of respondents indicating a need for improvement in education and awareness in the development of an effective stewardship ministry.

- The word "stewardship" simply means to manage someone else's property. For the Christian, the implication is clear: Scripture proclaims everything belongs to God (Psalm 24:1), so everything we have is managed for the Lord, including our very bodies and spiritual gifts.
- Christian stewardship requires the practical obedience and commitment for the administration of everything under

the church's control, and everything God entrusts to us for the building of God's kingdom on earth.

- The need for an annual stewardship service to consecrate oneself and possessions to God is helpful to remind and challenge congregations to acknowledge God as the owner and authority over us and church property.

Figure 11

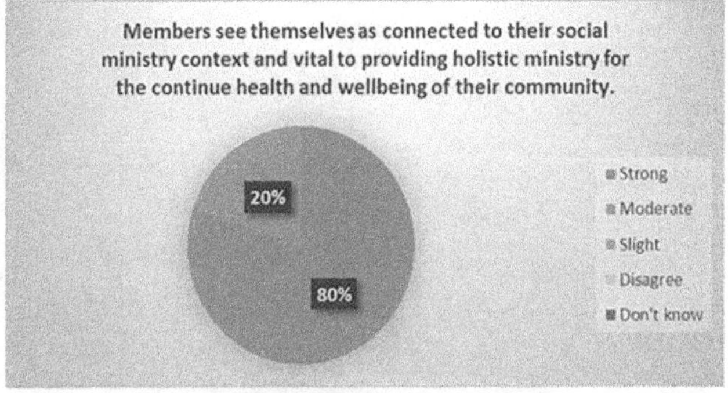

Outward Community Focused

Survey findings indicated 80% of respondents strongly agreed members were connected to their social ministry context in providing holistic ministry for the continued health and well-being of the community. Findings also indicated that 20% of respondents moderately agreed that their churches were connected to their social ministry context and provided holistic ministry for their community.

- For the most part, social ministries normally do not include emphasis on Christian faith sharing because of restrictions on public-sponsored funding, and evangelism ministries oftentimes are limited and do not focus on material needs. However, the church today must be mission-focused, with both evangelism and social ministry taking place along similar lines of ministry.
- For churches working toward church growth, it is vitally important that they conduct a needs assessment of the community to determine how the church can meet the needs of their community, which ultimately will attract more families, youth, and children.

Figure 12

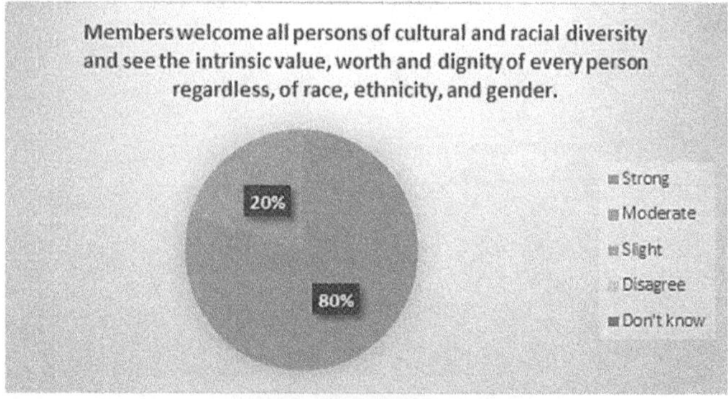

Cultural and Racial Diversity

Eighty percent of survey respondents strongly agreed that their congregation welcomes all persons regardless of culture or racial identity, and they see the intrinsic value, worth, and dignity of every person regardless of race, ethnicity, and gender. Another 20% of respondents moderately agreed with the proposition that their congregation welcomes cultural and racial diversity.

- We live in a global society consisting of persons from all racial and ethnic backgrounds, and churches must always be attentive to hidden forms of prejudice and stereotypes that people bring to cultures or races that may result in discrimination.
- Houses of worship are reflective of the growing cultural and religious diversity in the United States; however, there is a greater need than ever for people of all religious affiliations and nationalities to learn from each other, adapt, and grow toward a better understanding of the cultural and religious differences brought to ministry contexts.

Figure 13

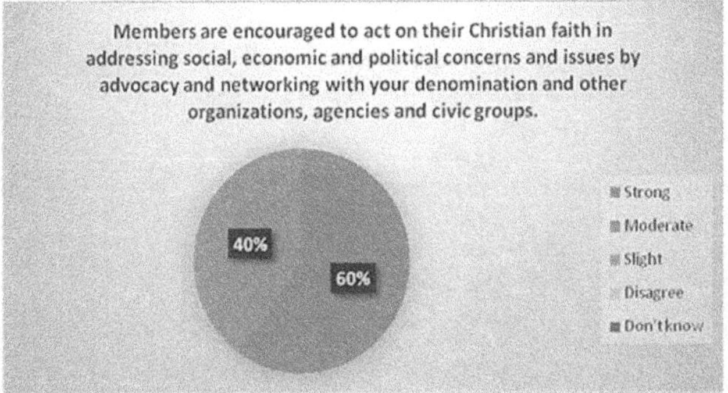

Social Action, Advocacy, and Networking

More than 60% of respondents strongly agreed their congregation membership acts on their Christian faith in social action, advocacy, and networking. On the other hand, 40% of respondents moderately agreed with the same question.

- It is vitally important that congregations act upon their Christian faith in addressing social, economic, and political issues in the community, although the question exists of whether they are supported by their denominations and other organizations, agencies, and civic groups.
- Although the churches surveyed, as well as many other congregations, are committed to serving the needy and advocating for justice in Christ's name, the focus of their ministry is mainly based on meeting social needs with no explicit attempt to bring those they serve to Christ or nurturing the faith of others. Often this kind of approach to social action is based on a theological understanding that identifies evangelism with doing good works with limited measurable results for growing the kingdom of God.

Figure 14

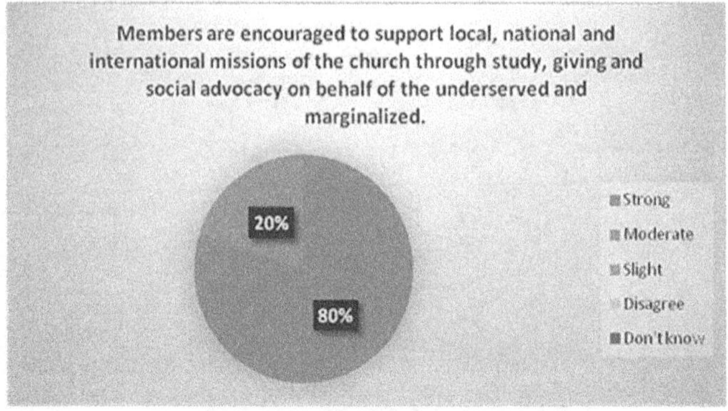

Missions (Local/Global)

Eighty percent of survey respondents strongly agreed that members are encouraged to support local, national, and international missions of the church through study, giving, and social advocacy on behalf of the underserved and marginalized; 20% of respondents indicated a moderate response to support and encouragement of missions on the local, national, and global level.

- While living out the example of Christ is essential to authenticate the gospel message, evangelism requires the proclamation of the gospel message of Jesus Christ to both believers and non-believers (Mark 16:15; 1 Peter 2:9). Global missions involve the task of seeing the Church established among every people so that every group has trained believers who can then reach out to other people through evangelism while demonstrating Christ's love (Romans 1:5; Revelation 7:9).

- Completing mission-related tasks involves a commitment of human and material resources and spiritual gifts, as well as equipping people for many different roles. Is it also something the church must envision itself doing, both for local and global missions, in the task of reaching out to families, children, and youth.

More Thoughts for Consideration

As we consider the above results, there are a few other important factors to note. The original health and faithfulness survey questions, as presented by the American Baptist Churches of New Jersey (ABC-NJ) when the project began in 2013, vary slightly from the ones that were used in this survey.

The above survey findings undoubtedly address issues and concerns related to factors that contribute to church growth and decline, but there are still other factors that must be considered and addressed if churches are to grow and thrive through the existing generation and beyond. In the next chapter, we will look at new realities, including the "digital divide" and race relations, to assess the dilemma of what the church must do in order to reach an ever-changing world for Christ.

Questions for Reflection

1. In the beginning of this chapter, the life cycle of a congregation was discussed. What stage of this cycle is your own congregation currently in?

2. Study the two line graphs that outline the survey results on church health and faithfulness. After a brief assessment, determine where you would place your own congregation on those graphs for each health and faithfulness factor.

5

Facing New Realities of the Future

Open for me the gates of the righteous; I will
enter and give thanks to the Lord.
Psalm 118:19

By now, we've reached a critical juncture in our assessment of church health and faithfulness. We've examined various statistics related to declining church membership in the United States, as well as biblical and historical factors that impact a church's ability to thrive and remain healthy. In the last chapter, we examined survey results from participating congregations and how they translate into an overall assessment of church health and faithfulness. We examined the life cycle of a congregation – the stages of birth, formation, stability, decline, and death – and particularly how they relate to the conditions of the surveyed congregations. As we discovered, all surveyed churches are unquestionably in various stages of transition.

Now, we must explore the answer to a very important question: what does it all mean for these congregations, and the 21st-century church in general, as it continues to face new realities in an ever-changing world? As we've learned thus far, it is an indisputable fact that numerous factors are driving the need for the church to successfully adapt in order to reach the world for Christ. In short, the church can no longer afford to remain still, or inert.

Dictionary.com defines the word "inert" as "having no power of action, motion, or resistance"; the word "inertia" is defined as "inertness, especially with regard to effort, motion, action, and the like; inactivity; sluggishness" – both powerful descriptors of the church's lack of mobility in addressing the need for relevant change. James Spencer, Vice President and COO of the Moody Center in Northfield, Massachusetts, speaks of the effects of inertia in the church in a May 2020 online article, "Inertia: Confronting Our Tendency to Continue Unchanged"[50]:

> ...inertia's effects can carry us forward when we should really be changing direction. I realized that I needed to learn how to resist "the urge to sustain institutions or programs that God has used despite the fact that God is no longer using them"....
>
> To the extent that the body of Christ is unwilling or unable to discern the Spirit, inertia has the potential to be a new power that stands in opposition to God and what He seeks to accomplish in the world.

Because our churches are clearly in crisis, this notion of inertia and its paralyzing effect cannot be emphasized enough. In light of the survey results we examined, however, the mission of Spirit-led change and its implementation within the body of Christ can be addressed by considering four realities that the church must acknowledge and effectively deal with if it is to remain healthy and faithful: ***the intergenerational gap***; ***the digital divide***; ***race, ethnicity, and gender***; and ***moral and ethical issues***.

The Intergenerational Gap

"The Millennial's Guide to the Older Generations," a 2015 blog post published by Pittsburgh Theological Seminary,[51] attempted to address commonly associated reasons why millennial pastors and church leaders (those born between early 1980 and early 2000) struggle to relate to or understand older church members. A few of these reasons include:

1. *Older generations lack technology skills.* Older church members are often intimidated by technology and in fact don't even know how to talk to their own grandchildren, who often spend most of their days staring at some type of digital screen;
2. *Older generations are unaccustomed to change.* As opposed to millennials, who have grown up with change as a swift and natural part of life, many older church members have spent most of their lives in the same homes, at the same jobs, and within the same church congregations. They're often loyal

to institutions and cannot understand how or why younger people change jobs or churches so easily; and

3. *Older generations consider truth differently.* Older church members tend to research and verify the truth by consulting experts (typically in print form), while millennials think of truth in terms of group-sourced opinions or online observations – an approach that not only forces reality to become an issue of relativity but ultimately has significant implications for standards of biblical authority.

A 2020 Barna research survey titled "Five Trends Shaping the Next Season of Next Gen Discipleship," examined the flip side of the generational gap and the dilemma of how older pastors can successfully relate and minister to younger congregation members. The online survey, taken among a selection of Protestant senior pastors between March 20, 2020, and July 30, 2020, examined prominent challenges facing the younger generation of Millennials and how the church must address them:

1. *The church must help younger generations wisely navigate screen time.* Recent reports confirm that Millennials and members of Gen Z (individuals born between 1996 and 2015) significantly increased daily screen usage during the COVID-19 pandemic. Barna research indicated that more than 85% of pastors surveyed were concerned about the shift, as they had been contending with the issue of growing, excessive device usage among young people even before the pandemic and social distancing became a necessary part of life. A similar percentage of pastors

surveyed (86%) reported that, despite this growing trend, their church had yet to develop a plan on how to teach wise technology use and its impact on spiritual growth among youth;

2. *The church must integrate its response to injustice into children and youth ministry.* Even before the age of racial injustice and inequity began to dominate the conversation in the United States, earlier Barna research studies demonstrate that teens and young adults are keen to investigate stories of injustice and are hopeful to become a positive change in the world. Although many young people look to the church for answers to some of the difficult questions surrounding injustice, many others also believe that the church does not have the best reputation for addressing these issues;
3. *The church must address loneliness and anxiety among young adults.* Despite being the most digitally connected generation, research reveals that teens and young adults are often prone to feelings of loneliness and anxiety, particularly in dealing with the psychological stress of the COVID-19 pandemic. It is a situation that leaves young adults ripe for meaningful connection, as 19% of 18 to 35-year-old Christians agree that friends are missing from their worship community; and
4. *The church must support and encourage resilient disciples to grow their faith.* Millennials and Gen Z members are less likely than older generations to be connected to a church, and it's no surprise that the church dropout rate among 18 to 25-year-olds has increased significantly within the

> past decade, up from 59% to 64%. Research data also finds that many members of younger generations do not view church as being personally relevant (59%) or believe that they can find God elsewhere (48%). Considering these statistics, the church must invest in the process of listening to the "resilient disciples", or the 10% of Christian twenty-somethings who have countered the trend of leaving the church, in order to successfully help other young adults in their spiritual walk and foster a holistic, lasting faith.

Certainly, the concept of a generational "gap" and how to overcome differences between the young and old is nothing new. In American society, this gap stems largely from the widely accepted norm of age separation as is most fundamentally seen in the U.S. school system. This type of separation translates into the same segregation in churches, everything from children's "church" to youth ministries and Bible studies, that are held apart from adult activities. However, this practice of segregation has often been responsible for age-related misunderstandings, relational difficulties, and even prejudice within the walls of the church.

In recent decades, the challenge for congregations to bridge the generation gap has given way to the formation of *intergenerational ministry* – that is, a ministry that strives to bridge church unity with the unity of entire families, for the purpose of building cross-generational relationships. From high school students serving meals to shut-in seniors to age-integrated Bible studies, this type of ministry can help members from various generations not only invest in one another but transform the church into an intergenerational, Christ-centered community.

According to *Christianity Today*, successful intergenerational ministries – regardless of teaching, worship, or outreach – can close the gap by implementing the following principles:

1. *Age integration*, by intentionally constructing teams of people from varying age groups rather than separated according to age or grade level;
2. *Generational understanding*, by fostering relationships that reduce typical intergenerational conflict or misunderstanding;
3. *Household integration*, by mainstreaming singles, widows, and other heads-of-household with nuclear families; and
4. *Parental responsibility for faith development*, by equipping and encouraging parents to take more of a primary role in their children's faith education and spiritual walk.[52]

The Digital Divide

Certainly, the evolution of the digital divide has become a timely and necessary issue to consider over the course of the past few years, as societies around the world continue to transition into the realm of online socializing, entertainment, and telecommuting. But what exactly does this "divide" mean for the church?

As we discussed in the previous section, part of the answer lies in the dilemma of the generational gap and its impact on the future of the church. While younger generations of technologically savvy churchgoers have been born and raised in the digital age, immersed in everything from social media to online gaming. Many older congregation members including pastors and lay leaders struggle with the task of simply opening an Internet browser on a computer. Unquestionably, this technological gap separating the "literate" from the "illiterate" has become increasingly polarizing in how older church members relate to those belonging to younger generations, many of whom, as we've already learned, are leaving the church in greater numbers each year. Whether it likes it or not, the church has been catapulted into the digital age and must learn how to navigate within its boundaries if it is to reach young people for Christ.

For many congregations, however, the transition to the digital divide is not as easy as it may seem. The U.S. Department of Commerce, National Telecommunications and Information Administration (NTIA) defines the digital divide as "any uneven distribution in the access to, use of, or impact of information and communications technologies (ICT) between any number of distinct groups, which can be defined based on social, geographical, or geopolitical criteria or otherwise."[53] Specifically, many smaller churches located in rural, more isolated areas, or churches in certain socioeconomic communities – particularly lower income, African American and Latino communities – with less access to Internet services or computers and other digital devices, are often at risk of being left behind in the evolution of technological advancement. The disparity has become so prevalent that organizations such as the National Black Church Initiative have implemented projects to address it:

> The faith community recognizes how critically important it is to have a technically wise and wired congregation. Access to technology and to IT education is critically important for the church to be on the cutting edge of this technological revolution. NBCI's initiative has two primary goals:
>
> - To make sure that every person in America, regardless of age or station in life, has access to technology.
> - To make sure that IT education opportunities are open to all regardless of income or race.
>
> We plan to work with large technology companies such as Microsoft, Yahoo, and Google to ensure that we fulfill our mission.[54]

The onset of the COVID-19 pandemic became another example of the digital divide when, in the spring of 2020, thousands of congregations around the world suddenly closed their doors to in-person meetings and Sunday morning services. Churches that were not as technologically advanced found themselves facing the challenge of how to minister and stay connected to its members throughout the challenging time, with many resorting to simply holding church services via telephone conference calls. More technologically "savvy" congregations, however, transitioned seamlessly into social distancing mode by holding online services through mediums such as Zoom, YouTube, or Facebook Live, and kept members apprised of events by posting church bulletins and updates on social media or their websites.

Churches that were able to remain digitally connected throughout the onset of the pandemic did more than cater to their congregants, however. According to a recent survey, "Giving in Faith: How Coronavirus Has Widened the Digital Divide," conducted by the online platform Givelify, 55% of faith-based organizations, particularly technologically savvy ones, experienced consistent or increased giving levels during the pandemic. In the initial days of COVID-19's spread throughout the United States in 2020, between March 15 and April 18, donations on the Givelify mobile app nearly doubled, and organizations with a strong online presence, such as their websites or social media outlets, saw a whopping 533% more in donations than organizations without one. And according to individuals surveyed, approximately 92% of donors indicated that they would continue to give primarily online and through mobile devices even after the pandemic ended.[55]

Other factors contributing to a church's limited or non-existent online presence may include a lack of time among church staff and volunteers, a lack of financial resources, and a lack of overall interest in technological development within the congregation itself. The need for a church to at least maintain and update a functioning, interactive website, however, is clearly a task that requires some level of investment for the relevant, 21st-century congregation that seeks to increase its impact on community outreach. According to Bill Nix, CEO of Axletree Media, the barriers are low in the quest for simple, online development of ministry resources that more churches should take advantage of:

> With the low cost of online technology today, any size congregation can build and maintain a helpful website. Plus, updating a website has become so easy that no church needs to feel like it lacks the technological savvy to have a presence on the Internet.[56]

Race, Ethnicity, and Gender

Trayvon Martin…Ahmaud Arbery...George Floyd...Breonna Taylor...Jacob Blake…Michael Brown. At the time of this writing, it would be difficult to find an American citizen who has not heard of at least one of these names – and for good reason. The tragedies behind these once-ordinary citizens' shocking stories – and for most of them, their untimely deaths – have catapulted our society into a new, unprecedented conversation about race, racism, and racial inequality, resulting in everything from nationwide protests and marches to social media campaigns, led by everyone from high-profile celebrities and government officials to grassroots organizers in every major city throughout America.

But while a series of high-profile events have brought about a seemingly heightened awareness of racism, there is, unfortunately, one place where the conversation remains far too silent: the Christian church. A September 2020 article from *Race Today,* an online Barna Research briefing, revealed that just 43% of self-identified Christians who claim that faith is very important to their lives acknowledge the problem of racial injustice. What's more, there has been a dramatic increase in the number of Christians who believe that race is not a problem "at all" in the United States, up from 11% in 2019 to 19% in 2020. The disparity becomes even clearer when examining the 2020 survey results based on race and ethnicity, where over 78% of self-identified black Christians believe that the United States has a history of minority oppression, compared to 63% of Hispanics and just 48% of white Christians surveyed.[57]

Arguably, the church's responsibility to address the matter of racial inequality must begin within its own congregations, consisting of a frank – and likely difficult – look at how factors that foster inequality are composed within its denominational structure or general practices, down to the very curriculum used in many church-run schools. In his book, *Divided by Faith*, sociologist Michael Emerson argued that evangelicals "likely do more to perpetuate the racial divide than to tear it down" because of the church's tendency to worship in racially segregated congregations. Emerson also suggested that racial reconciliation would follow if more Christians practiced worshipping together in multicultural congregations.[58]

Although that concept has been widely received in evangelical circles since the book's publication in 2000, a recent survey completed by Duke University among U.S. congregations suggests that the formation of multicultural congregations isn't quite as simple as it may seem. While the number of churches defined as "multicultural," or those with at least one out of five members with a minority background, grew from just 6% in 1998 to 16% in 2019, the diversity of the congregations themselves changed only slightly, from 16% to 21%, and in fact decreased between 2012 and 2019.

What's more, white membership in multicultural congregations remained virtually unchanged at approximately 50%, from 1998 to 2019.

"Integrated churches are tough things," says Keith Moore, a black pastor in Montgomery, Alabama. "When you see both African Americans and Caucasian Americans [in a church], it's more than likely to have a Caucasian pastor. I think it's sometimes more difficult for whites to look at a Black pastor and see him as their authority. That's a tough call for many." Moore also believes that, for African Americans to integrate into a multicultural congregation, they are generally expected to abandon their culture and traditions in order to "fit in."[59] Many of these cultural differences, which often exist between white and African American churches, include length of church service time, formal versus casual dress, and worship styles.

Korie Little Edwards, author of the book *The Elusive Dream: The Power of Race in Interracial Churches,* believes that African American churchgoers often lose out in the course of attempting to integrate and that the answer doesn't necessarily lie in the practice of integration itself. "The pain people experience is not feeling like they're accepted for who they are, not being able to be themselves, not being able to worship how they want to worship.... I would argue that the goal shouldn't be diversity. Rather, all churches are called to be places of justice, uplifting the oppressed. That is what the Christian faith is. All churches, regardless of their racial and ethnic composition, should be like that. And then you can move toward integration."[60]

Inasmuch that is lacking in the church's ability to address the problems of racial inequality, sadly, it continues to remain relatively silent on the issue of gender inequality as well. It is certainly no secret that, while great strides have been made over the past century, there is much work that remains to be done regarding the disparities between men and women, the roles they play, the trend towards inequalities and injustices, and how the church can be a catalyst for reconciliation regarding gender equality in the United States.

Like racial inequality, gender inequality can be examined on an *internal* and *external* basis – that is, how inequality exists first within the church and then branching out to the broader consideration of how and where it exists outside the church in general society. Within the church, there has undoubtedly been a longstanding debate over the boundaries of gender roles that stems largely from a variance in biblical interpretation on the subject. ***Complementarian theology***, or the beliefs that men and women are equal in worth but hold separate roles within the church and family structure, is based primarily on scriptures such as Genesis 2:28 ("It is not good for the man to be alone. I will make a helper suitable for him") and Titus 2:3-5 ("Likewise, teach the older women to be reverent in the way they live… Then they can urge the younger women to love their husbands and children, to be self-controlled and pure, to be busy at home, to be kind, and to be subject to their husbands, so that no one will malign the word of God"). Complementarianism is also characterized by the tenet that only men should hold church leadership positions (although women may hold positions of authority over other women) and the patriarchal philosophy that the father or husband is head of the household. ***Egalitarianism theology,*** by contrast, adheres those scriptures such as Galatians 3:28 ("There is neither Jew nor Gentile, neither slave nor free, nor is there male and female, for you are all one in Christ Jesus") support the beliefs that both men and women can hold leadership positions of any type within the church, that both spouses are equally responsible for the family, and that marriage is a partnership of two equals.

Although both views offer scriptural support, who holds which view often runs along denominational lines, with many complementarians stemming from Southern Baptist, Presbyterian, Lutheran, or Reformed denominations, while egalitarians can often be found within the ranks of Episcopalian, Mennonite, or United Methodist denominations. Although the issue of women in church leadership has long been a source of contention within the church, there has been evidence of change in recent decades. A 2016 survey conducted by Barna research revealed that, although statistics vary within church factions, 62% of practicing Christians, or those who attend a religious service at least once a month and who self-identify as a Christian, are accepting of a female pastor, with the least accepting percentage of churchgoers being among evangelicals at just 39%. To that end, the percentage of female Protestant senior pastors (9%) in the United States has in fact tripled from 25 years ago.[61]

When it comes to American society, however, or considering the external basis of the subject, it is a potentially oppressive patriarchal worldview that continues to affect the perception of women as being secondary citizens. Since the United States' founding more than three centuries ago, women have fought for, and won, equal rights regarding everything from the right to vote and own property, from sitting on jury panels to holding public offices. As has been notably highlighted in recent years throughout the rise of the #metoo movement, the same patriarchal system serves to restrict a woman's ability to be their own advocate in instances of rape, sexual assault, or sexual discrimination. The U.S. also continues to address issues such as employment discrimination and equal pay for women.

CBE (Christians for Biblical Equality) International is a Minnesota-based, nonprofit ministry that seeks to bridge the gap in addressing the needs of women who have been victims of abuse, gender-based violence, and human trafficking, both around the world as well as the United States. Through collaboration with churches, schools, and other ministry partners from more than 100 denominations in 65 countries, CBE International is a leading force in addressing gender inequality within the church. Since 1989, CBE has offered a variety of print and online resources, including both adult and youth curriculum, as well as annual conferences, in support of its mission to advance a future where "all believers are freed to exercise their gifts for God's glory and purposes, with the full support of their Christian communities."[62] No doubt, as it seeks to support women who have been victimized by gender inequality, CBE's widespread ministry presence and the tools it provides certainly offer a model for other churches looking to provide outreach in this critical issue affecting contemporary culture.

But perhaps the simplest, and yet most profound, solution for the church in its task of becoming a relevant, equitable voice in the world and ultimately reaching others for Christ, lies in the words of Paula Frances Price as penned in a 2019 blog post:

> To be one in Christ, we need to allow for differing theologies and learn how to engage in healthy debate. But differing beliefs should never allow for harmful practices. God created all women and men in his image, and as such, no theology should allow for practices that harm and abuse women.[63]

Moral and Ethical Issues

It's certainly no secret that mankind is living in increasingly uncertain times. From cultural and societal changes to political upheavals, the world today seems more unstable now than ever before. In the mist of it all, moral and ethical values continue to erode and evolve, as evidenced by the rising trends toward gun violence, drug use, suicide, and racial and ethnic injustices. Therein lies yet another important question for the church: how must we respond to the myriad of moral and ethical issues in contemporary society today? What should be the church's response on matters of divorce, pornography, same-sex marriage, and transgenderism? How about war, abortion, and global warming? Capital punishment and euthanasia? Obedience to government and other civil authorities?

Steven D. West of The Gospel Coalition defines Christian ethics as being "guided by God's revelation in Scripture above other systems of thought as it seeks to love God and neighbor in every moral and ethical issue," and that "the highest ethical duty of a Christian is the same as the greatest commandment: love God and love your neighbor."[64] While that certainly sounds simple – and accurate – enough, the fact is that the church remains divided on how to handle many issues. Why? Sadly, contemporary Christians, even as they worship together week in and week out and profess to be one body in Christ, are painfully split on their views regarding key subjects.

Part of the reason for this disparity lies in the variance of authoritative sources regarding ethics and morality. While it certainly can't be denied that most Christians want to truly know and understand God's will as it relates to morals and ethics, a discrepancy exists as to where the source, or sources, of that understanding comes from. Many believers place emphasis on the Bible as the primary source of authority, even as there are differing beliefs over which biblical texts are more authoritative than others, as well as interpretational differences affected by familial upbringing, racial, ethnic, and socioeconomic factors. Other Christians tend to place emphasis on dogmatic teachings or church leadership as authoritative sources, while still others rely on the personal, inner convictions of the Holy Spirit to guide their decisions and convictions.

However, there is a growing divide among believers on which stance to take regarding certain issues such as human rights, abortion, racial and social justice. Many Christians increasingly face a generalized fear of further polarization within the church if they do take a stand at all. This hesitation among believers has become a trend not only within church congregations but also in Christian schools, colleges, and seminaries. Consequently, many Christians either keep their beliefs to themselves or stick within circles of like-minded people. Another reason for church inconsistency is that many believers are simply not equipped to address certain contemporary moral dilemmas. For example, should a Christian handle an invitation to a gay relative's wedding ceremony? What should be their response when a co-worker confides that they've cheated on ten years' worth of tax returns?

When Tom Gilson, author of the online article, "Equipping Christians to Think Clearly About the Political, Economic and Moral Issues of Our Day," conducted a Facebook poll asking participants if they could recall ever hearing church sermons that specifically addressed practical ethical dilemmas, more than 57% of them responded no. Gilson asserted five primary reasons why these survey results should be a concern to Christians:

1. If churches aren't teaching us the right thing, who is?
2. As new questions and dilemmas continually come our way, the church needs guidance in determining what is right;
3. It's not enough to simply do right, the church needs to be able to *explain* what's good about doing right;
4. The church, particularly youth, needs an entire community of moral support behind doing what's right; and
5. Without a stronger stance on moral and ethical issues, the church could miss out on its mission.

"It isn't enough to preach what's in the Bible," states Gilson. "It never was. We've got to connect it with day-to-day life. If the gospel we preach doesn't address people's questions, it won't touch their hearts. Which questions? These days, moral issues sit at the top of the list."[65]

So, where should the church start in addressing these issues? According to Steven West, despite variations in schools of thought, Christians need to make serious effort in applying a more fundamental interpretation of biblical principles to matters of ethics and morality:

> The Bible makes it clear that things are right or wrong in relationship to God's character. Thus, morality is objective, and we must obey God's commands.... There are, of course, an enormous number of practical ethical issues that Christians face today. Some issues in certain societies are relatively recent, like legalized abortion and same-sex marriage. Other issues are more universal and perennial, like general sexual issues or the justification of self-defense and war. Sometimes God has spoken clearly and directly about an ethical issue (e.g., do not steal), but there are other topics that could not have been directly addressed in the Bible (e.g., issues that require contemporary technology, like genetic engineering or in vitro fertilization). Even when the Bible does not specifically speak to an issue, there are biblical principles that can be relied upon to make an informed moral judgment.[66]

***

As we reflect on critical realities facing the church today – the intergenerational gap; the digital divide; race, ethnicity, and gender; and relevant moral and ethical issues – we are once again left with the question: what do these realities mean for a church seeking to become a healthier, more faithful congregation? It's time now for us to turn again to our surveyed churches, where, as we re-examine their profiles, we will determine the ideal next steps in missional planning for church growth and faithfulness.

Questions for Reflection

1. Do you consider your congregation to be intergenerational? Why or why not?

2. How "technologically savvy" is your church? Does it maintain a website or social media presence? Why or why not? Do you believe this is an important factor in the relevance of the church today? Why or why not?

3. Do you consider your church to be racially and ethnically diverse? If not, what are some of the ways it could improve this type of community outreach?

4. What do you believe is the overall theology of your congregation, complementarian or egalitarian? Depending on your answer, how can it reach other churches with a differing viewpoint?

5. What do you feel are some of the most pressing moral and ethical issues the church faces today? Why?

6

Missional Planning for Church Growth and Faithfulness

"For I know the plans I have for you," declares the Lord,
"plans to prosper you and not to harm you,
plans to give you hope and a future."
Jeremiah 29: 11

A clear-cut case advocating the need for change within the church, amid unprecedented challenges, has been outlined so far in this book. From addressing age-old cultural and social dilemmas to tackling new, evolving realities, there's no doubt about it, the church has much to think and pray about these days. And as many congregations throughout the United States seek answers on how to navigate their next steps for growth and faithfulness, we will ultimately circle back to our original quest of studying the profiled churches and answer the question: how have *they* been faring in these challenging times?

Before we do that in the next and final chapter, though, we must ponder another very important question: how does the church generally go about the business of actually *planning* growth and faithfulness? For the congregation who is intentionally seeking to become more missional in its impact on the communities around them and thereby ultimately reaching their neighbors for Christ, where does the process even begin? The answer fundamentally lies in three components that must be put into place for this to occur: ***a good support team, an annual assessment,*** and ***an action plan.***

Establish a Support Team

The first step in the process for growing a healthy and faithful congregation is to establish a congregational support team. By overall definition, a support team assists leadership in addressing both the short and long-term needs of a congregation, everything from missions to hospitality needs, from finances to church building projects. Support teams are also essential for helping to implement or improve outreach ministries in neighboring communities, particularly in congregations where leaders are already stretched thin for time and resources and have become increasingly dependent on lay leaders' initiatives, a scenario that has become all-too-familiar in many U.S. churches. According to a 2020 Barna survey, "Better Together," more than 68% of pastors surveyed believed that laity must take on greater responsibility for a church to become healthier, although only 50% believed that their church was proficient at developing new leaders.[67] Accordingly, it must also be said that assembling a good, reliable support team is a process that can lead to the development of strong church leadership from within a congregation's own ranks. In a June 2019 blog post,

"10 Truths of Churches That Do a Great Job With Leadership Development," Leadership Network asserted that the leading success factor among studied churches that effectively planted new campuses or had the greatest impact on their cities was the practice of strong leadership development. Within that practice, several of the ten identified "fruitfulness" factors among the studied congregations included the facts that each church focused on building leaders from within, the recognition of apprenticeship and ongoing coaching as part of their success model, and a strong commitment to staff leadership development.[68]

It can certainly be said that a successful ministry is rarely the result of a single person's efforts, and that accomplishing God's purpose for a congregation flows best out of teamwork. To that end, in the process of assembling a support team, it's important to convey the "all-in" mentality and belief that scripture calls every single member of the body of Christ to serve in some way, shape, or form (Galatians 5:13-14) and that ministry is comprised of everyone, not just a select few. Within the family of God's people, each and every member has not just an obligation but a privilege to serve Him by serving others. Good support teams, and when possible, even the subcommittees that oversee them, are comprised of spiritually mature helpers, encouragers, and intercessors that are committed to serving the needs of a growing congregation.

Practically speaking, a quality support team should ideally and intentionally include diversity that represents not just the entire congregation but the surrounding community the church is seeking to reach. The inclusion of these individuals is so important, in fact, that a congregation might also consider inviting a community member or two to become part of the support team in an effort to promote a healthy, "external" perspective on the church's mission and goals.

It is also important to assess whether a congregation which may have been historically resistant to change is even ready for the component of a good support team. Support team members should be encouraged to explore open, honest conversations about whether they're willing to truly operate as a team, to identify potential leadership barriers, to respect the opinions and perspectives of others, to understand the limitations that general attitudes place on the success of the overall ministry, and whether they are willing to look at change for the sake of church growth. Scheduling regular times for collective team prayer will keep the progress on track and the congregational vision clear and in focus. If necessary, an outside consultant can also help with a frank review of what steps a support team can and should take to help move the church to the next critical level.

Conduct an Annual Assessment

The second important factor, or "action" step, for missional planning and the promotion of a congregation's health and faithfulness is to conduct a congregational assessment. Simply put, an assessment can help identify a church's strengths as well as areas that require attention. Assessments also provide an excellent means for accountability to God and each other. For the local church, this requires taking the time to ask the right questions and ensure that the start of its journey towards increased growth, health, and faithfulness begins in a good place. This is especially important because if the journey doesn't begin with the right steps, churches can miss out on pivotal information essential to accurately understanding their present condition.

Annual review via a church health and faithfulness assessment allows pastors, lay leaders, and members alike to measure progress – or discover the lack of it. By taking the time to analyze various aspects of the present work, we can accurately see what's effective and what is not. Neglected ministry areas can be brought into focus and become either a source of encouragement to improve or an opportunity to address important factors the congregation needs to more closely address.

Conducting a church health assessment can be an intimidating thing; it often forces us to face unpleasant realities, and the findings might explore some demanding questions not only of the congregation but of ourselves. Yet, growth and improvement only come when we take stock of how things really are, and if we fail to review and assess where we are, we will most certainly miss out on opportunities for spiritual growth.

Before a congregation effectively begins an assessment, there are a few identifying questions that must be answered. How does the church perceive itself in terms of structure and makeup? Is it a traditional, mainline congregation? Is it evangelical? Something in the middle? Exactly where is the church at the beginning of this assessment period, and how does it plan to move forward from the starting point? A congregation must establish and affirm its identity before an assessment process can even begin.

Ideally, assessments or surveys should be lay driven, not pastor or leadership driven, and as many congregants as possible should be encouraged to participate. Several factors should also be kept in mind in the course of preparing and conducting an effective congregational assessment:

1. *Communicate the reason for, and value of, the assessment.*

   From the onset, pastors and church leaders should clearly convey to congregation members that an assessment is not intended to imply blame or push guilt on others, nor is it intended to promote an agenda or attack existing ministries in any way. Rather, it is a vehicle with which to make an honest evaluation of the church's strengths and weaknesses and determine which direction the entire body needs to go from the present onward;

2. *Decide on the appropriate assessment tool and make the assessment widely available for participants.*

   Although formal, written surveys are the most common type of church assessment, assessments can also be done through a series of formal, conversational interview questions. Whichever method is used, it should be made readily available to all willing participants of the assessment. Paper copies of written surveys should be placed conveniently in or near high-traffic areas such as the sanctuary or Sunday School classrooms, and if possible, available for download through the church website, or even sent to participants through direct mail. Interview assessments should be conducted by two or three diverse focus groups in order to ensure the best representation of the entire church body, ideally at least ten percent of the congregation. The health and faithfulness survey found in this book can also be a highly effective assessment tool for congregants;

3. *Use assessment results constructively.*

   Although assessments are designed to identify strengths as well as weaknesses, many church leaders tend to immediately focus on the weaknesses or challenges, that must be corrected. What perhaps could be a more positive and effective starting point, however, is to encourage the congregation to celebrate all that God has already done and discuss how the church can continue to improve and expand on those successes; and

4. *Establish a habit of routine assessment.*

   All too often, many church congregations fall into ruts, developing practices over time that may not be the most effective methods of conducting church business or community outreach. By developing a culture of consistent assessment and appraisal, whether it's on a monthly, quarterly, or annual basis, congregations can avoid these habitual, potentially unhealthy, ruts.

Establish an Action Plan

Perhaps one of the most fundamentally important things a healthy and faithful congregation can do, as part of the universal body of Christ, is recognize the fact that it can and will be aligned with God's will to accomplish his purposes on earth if it makes itself available and willing for such. For that reason alone, it is crucial that a church establish a good action plan to help carry out those purposes.

Although many would argue against the need for the church to plan for future direction, there are far more practical as well as scriptural arguments supporting the need for church planning. God created mankind not just with the ability but the need to plan, and when it comes to the body of Christ, it could be further contended that forethought and planning are essential components of a healthy, successful, and thriving church. The act of planning helps a congregation:

1. *Anticipate Church Expenses.* When a congregation takes the time to plan for projected expenses, it not only establishes prudent spending habits but counts the cost of carrying out its mission and goals (The wisdom of the prudent is to give thought to their ways (Proverbs 14:8); (Suppose one of you wants to build a tower. Will he not first sit down and estimate the cost to see if he has enough money to complete it? (Luke 14:28);
2. *Avoid Unforeseen Challenges.* All too often, church leaders fall into the trap of following a path or practice that may seem right at the onset but can have unintended, or even harmful, consequences when failing to think all the steps through (A simple man believes anything, but a prudent man gives thought to his steps (Proverbs 14:15); and

3. *Enable God's Blessings by Seeking His Wisdom.* When a church's first objective is to seek God's will and what he desires to accomplish in and through the congregation, to make him the center of all planning, and then follow through on those plans, scripture makes clear there are numerous blessings that come with such a practice (Good judgment wins favor, but the way of the unfaithful leads to their destruction (Proverbs 13:15); (The plans of the diligent lead to profit as surely as haste leads to poverty (Proverbs 21:5). Godly planning in this manner helps keep us humbly returning to God for perspective rather than relying solely on the opinions or counsel of humans.

Creating an action plan builds on a congregation's established mission and values and answers three important questions: *Where are we now? Where are we going? How will we get there?* While developing an action plan, a congregation would do well to ponder a few other important questions: What are the unique advantages that exist within our church? What do our programs, services, or ministries do or deliver more effectively than other local organizations or ministries? What exceptional talents, gifts, and capabilities exist among the congregation members, and how can they best be utilized? Once those gifts and talents have been identified, it must be determined how they can and will be used to achieve congregational objectives by asking: What are the key activities on the congregational "to-do" list that we would like to carry out? What steps do we need to take to make them a reality? What is an ideal, and realistic, timeline for us to accomplish these steps? Breaking the list into short-term (30, 60, and 90-day) and long-term (6, 12, and 18-month, or even 3-5 year) objectives will provide a realistic picture of how and when they will ultimately be accomplished. Some examples of "action" items on an objective to-do list may include:

- To develop and improve the leadership abilities and potential of church staff;
- To improve and expand existing services to the congregation;
- To improve church fiscal operations; and
- To develop more community-based programs and services.

Once objectives have been defined, the next step is to develop a strategy on how to implement those objectives. OnStrategy, a Nevada-based consulting firm, asserts the following about strategic planning:

> Simply put, a strategic plan is the formalized road map that describes how your organization executes the chosen strategy. A plan spells out where an organization is going over the next year or more and how it is going to get there. A strategic plan is a management tool that serves the purpose of helping an organization do a better job, and it improves organizations because a plan focuses the energy, resources, and time of everyone in the organization in the same direction.

> Strategic planning does not have to be mysterious, complicated, or time-consuming. In fact, it should be quick, simple, and easily executed. Additionally, strategic planning is not just something you cross off your list of "to-dos"—you must create a culture of strategic thinking, so your strategic planning does not become an annual retreat but, instead, a part of daily decision making.

A good strategic plan achieves the following:

- Reflects the values of the organization;
- Clearly defines what is most important for achieving success;
- Assists everyone in daily decision making;
- Gets everyone on the same page focused and pulling in the same direction; and
- Creates a culture of strategic thinking.[69]

Ultimately, an action plan involves fleshing out a congregation's assets and assessing how they will be used to reach the communities around it for Christ. With that having been said, the fact that churches have the unique ability to play a crucial role in community development cannot be emphasized enough.

A commitment to greater community outreach should be a part of every healthy and faithful congregation's action plan, especially when outreach is done as part of a process called "asset mapping." John Kretzmann, co-author of *Building Communities From the Inside Out: A Path Toward Finding and Mobilizing a Community's Assets,* discusses the concept of asset mapping as an initiative that focuses primarily on the strengths and capabilities of a community, rather than its needs and deficits, as a way of bringing about necessary change, chiefly in lower income and working-class communities. Rather than focusing on a community's detriments such as prevalent drug use, homelessness, or crime and relying solely on external resources for help in rebuilding distressed communities. Effective asset mapping asserts that transformation will come about when these neighborhoods band together on the strengths, skills, and talents of their own citizens and their collective capacity for making meaningful, constructive contributions. At the heart of this concept is an "asset map," a community-based model that identifies and places the gifts, knowledge, resources, and values of local individuals, young and old alike, at the map's center. The foundational center, then branches out to a second level comprised of strong citizens' associations, organizations, clubs, and cultural groups. When these foundations have been established, the asset map can then identify solid institutions within a community such as strong businesses, schools, colleges, and medical institutions (see Appendix C). The asset map is in direct contrast to a "needs map," which tends to focus on deficits and problems primarily for the purpose of securing external or government assistance to address the prevailing weaknesses within a community.

To help engage both residents and neighborhood leaders in the process of designing an asset map, a custom-tailored "capacity inventory" survey can be drafted and implemented to help discover the skillsets, areas of expertise, and commitment levels among individuals within the community. Capacity inventory surveys should be taken by volunteers willing to perform in-person, door-to-door work within their own neighborhoods, for two important reasons: it promotes the highly effective, relationship-building process of "neighbors interviewing neighbors", and produces useful information that can be analyzed immediately, rather than information that tends to be simply stored away in a computer database for possible future use. Sample questions on a capacity inventory survey should include those that speak to an individual's "priority skills", or skillsets they have developed and feel most confident about:

1. What types of skills have you learned at home? In the community? In the workplace?
2. What types of cultural skills do you possess?
3. What type of enterprising or business skills or experience do you have?
4. Would you be willing to participate in a "local skills bank" to offer neighbor-to-neighbor assistance such as snow shoveling, babysitting, carpentry, or plumbing? Elder care or work with youth and teenagers?
5. If you would like to teach or have experience teaching, what would you like to teach? On the flip side, what would you like to learn about?
6. What are your interests and/or previous involvements with community organizations, schools, libraries, or churches? What type of neighborhood associations, groups, or clubs have you belonged to or would like to see established in the community? What would you be willing to be involved with in the future?

7. Do you possess any artistic abilities such as art, writing, drama, or music?
8. What do you feel are unserved or underserved consumer markets in the community?

Once the foundation of individual skillset contributions has been established, the next tier of the asset map is to focus on improving local institutions and organizations by asking: How can schools, libraries, and human service agencies contribute to community revitalization? The process of re-establishing relationships among these institutional leaders can lead to the discovery of a "treasure chest" of potentially untapped resources: i.e., would a school with ample space and equipment be willing to host various community events and activities? What type of additional services might an agency be able to provide that has never been offered before? Identifying these types of often overlooked resources and possibilities will help a community move forward with its rebuilding agenda much more quickly and efficiently.

As we examine the components of asset mapping and how it relates to the formation of a congregational action plan, it is clear to see how the local church is poised to have a significant impact on community development by assisting with, or even leading the way, in the implementation of an asset mapping initiative. Regardless of the strength or challenges of the surrounding communities, however, lay leaders and clergy alike should prioritize their long-term, active roles as community leaders, participants, volunteers, and servants, if they are serious about their church's mission to become a healthier and more faithful congregation.

But for all that can be said about planning, the actual implementation of an action plan is quite another task – in fact, most congregations have experienced, and will almost certainly experience, some measure of conflicts and challenges in the course of bringing about healthy, substantial change. Conflicts and challenges may prompt many individuals to want to give up. However, it's important to invest the proper time and effort necessary to see the finished product of a healthy and faithful congregation through to the end is of immeasurable and oftentimes of eternal importance. Carrying out an action plan means achieving pre-planned goals while remaining open and flexible to new opportunities that may manifest in the process. And as mentioned in the beginning of this chapter, successful ministry is never the result of one person's hard work; executing an action plan requires time, resources, and dedicated people who are willing to seek the Lord in prayer for continued direction and to humbly take corrective action, if necessary.

Summarily, then, it can be established that missional planning for church growth and faithfulness requires the presence of three critical components: a strong support team, an annual assessment, and an action plan. At the heart of the matter are the fundamental health factors: *clarity of mission and vision, worship, fellowship, leadership, discipleship,* and *values.* The faithfulness factors are: *evangelism, stewardship, community focus, diversity, social advocacy,* and *missions* which have been discussed and analyzed throughout this book. And have remained the primary theme of this project. They are the factors that we will address one final time as we return to the profiled congregations of St. Martin's Episcopal, St. Thomas A.M.E., Trinity United, New Horizon Christian Fellowship, First Baptist, and Fountain of Living Water – and take a revealing look at each church's successes, limitations, and challenges going forward in the midst of an ever-changing world.

Questions for Reflection

1. Has your church ever conducted a congregational assessment? Was it productive in identifying key strengths and weaknesses?

2. Do you consider lay leadership an important factor in a healthy and faithful church? Why or why not?

3. What are the steps your own congregation has taken to develop a strong support team?

4. Does your church have an action plan that maps out a strategy on how to move forward and accomplish its mission and objectives? If not, how would you begin the process of implementing one?

7

Celebrate Successes, Limitations, Observations, and New Beginnings

Forget the former things; do not dwell on the past.
See, I am doing a new thing! Now it springs
up; do you not perceive it?
I am making a way in the wilderness
and streams in the wasteland.
Isaiah 43:18-19 (NIV)

Without question, the health and faithfulness project as a whole has not been without its challenges. From the onset, selecting initial congregations that most closely represent the diverse array of churches throughout the United States was a painstaking process, as well as maintaining research on the six observed congregations even as they underwent their own changes throughout the years. For the churches themselves, those internal health and faithfulness challenges required true introspection, from leadership and congregational members alike, in order to effectively bring about change, particularly at the beginning of the COVID-19 pandemic.

Even now, it is a process that many of them continue to face today, as they decide what change will continue to look like in light of their challenges and limitations and, if they are to survive, how they will best utilize a newfound measure of post-COVID resiliency.

The project has also observed great successes, however, including its primary purpose of identifying the key elements required for health and faithfulness and how churches can strengthen or improve on those factors if they are serious about congregational growth, as well as the creation of a platform that will be used in sharing these critical findings and information with other congregations everywhere. In this final chapter, we will examine those challenges, limitations, and successes, and we will start by finally turning to the updated profiles of our surveyed congregations.

First Baptist Church

Like thousands of congregations throughout the United States, First Baptist has seen its share of considerable changes in recent months and years. Like many other congregations, is faced with the challenge of how to address them going forward.

While the world struggled to adapt to life throughout the COVID-19 pandemic in 2020, First Baptist remained vigilant to maintain regular worship services and stay connected to its congregants even as its building doors remained closed. Sunday services were held by teleconference, where churchgoers called in to participate in worship, listen to the live sermon, and offer prayer requests. Service information outlining a general theme, as well as a calendar of events and relevant Scripture passages, was prepared a full month in advance and sent by postal mail to each of the congregants in anticipation of upcoming services. Like other smaller congregations without more technologically advanced options, First Baptist was forced to resort to the simple means of telecommunication during the early days of the COVID-19 pandemic – a practice that demonstrated the dedication and resiliency of its members to stay connected during trying, unprecedented times.

First Baptist remains a congregation built on many strengths, one with a clear well-defined mission and vision statement. They present an unwavering dedication to its core values and maintain a welcoming environment for all visitors. One of its ongoing primary challenges lies in addressing the issues surrounding its aging congregation and the importance of drawing into its doors a younger, more diverse generation of individuals and families who will continue the work of the church. This dilemma becomes evident for the church in several ways. Although First Baptist continues to support overseas missions in regions such as Haiti, Russia, and the Congo, it is now faced with the quandary of how to reach out to the shifting demographics of diverse residents. Particularly, the emerging Hispanic and Asian-American communities, that now exists in its own backyard within Somerville, New Jersey. The question becomes how to invite them into its now predominantly African American congregation. There remains a 10% population of white American and 5% Asian American congregants.

Despite continuing to uphold its tradition of supporting missionaries and missionary programs in other countries, First

Baptist cannot be considered an evangelistic congregation in the sense of maintaining a team trained to spread the Gospel, build relationships, and "make disciples" within its own community. All of these are critical factors at the very heart of evangelistic outreach. Because of the high number of older congregants (most of whom are between 60 to 80 years of age) who have begun to experience mobility as well as health issues. First Baptist has become significantly limited in how extensively it fosters outreach to community members, particularly ones of diverse racial and ethnic groups. The dilemma of how to improve such outreach efforts must factor in not only the availability of volunteer manpower but the financial resources necessary to implement and maintain critical ministries and programs. Another great challenge facing First Baptist is how to address its aging congregation.

With the challenge of outreach to more diverse youth and families comes also the issue of implementing effective discipleship to not only train new, younger members in the faith but to help them identify and utilize their spiritual gifts for the kingdom of God. Like many other congregations both large and small, First Baptist must strive to address the overall disconnect between discipleship training and congregational life. There is a critical need to actively challenge and encourage younger participants to explore ways they can meaningfully serve within the church as well as the community at large.

Summarily, First Baptist faces four priorities in its current climate:

- ***Examination of its financial health,*** including its budget, income, and an exploration of online giving options, as well as exploration of developing partnerships with other churches and agencies in order to share the financial load of new and existing ministries;

- ***Increasing an online presence,*** primarily through the promotion of the church website and social media engagement for the purpose of spreading the Gospel and keeping local community residents informed about ministry programs and services;
- ***Greater development of targeted outreach,*** particularly outreach efforts to children, youth, and families, as well as outreach to members of varying racial and ethnic backgrounds, through strategic community assets mapping; and
- ***Exploring a renewed commitment to becoming a more Spirit-led congregation,*** including better equipping laity for the work of the ministry, as it faces its ongoing challenges.

Fountain of Living Water

"Close-knit family" might be one of the first terms that come to mind to describe Fountain of Living Water Church, but it is a family that has faced, and continues to face, many challenges since it formed decades ago in 1992. As of September 2021, it remains a small congregation consisting of approximately 40 adult members, most of whom range from 40 to 50 years old. Because the church currently does not have its own building, it rents space from First Baptist Church in Somerville, New Jersey.

The predominantly Hispanic congregation, whose members hail from regions such as Mexico, Puerto Rico, and the Dominican Republic, meets for one Sunday morning service at First Baptist. Although it streamed services remotely via Facebook Live during the onset of the COVID-19 pandemic, they lost several families to larger churches since it re-opened for in-person services in August of 2020. While the rebound has been slow but steady in re-gathering its members post-pandemic, Fountain of Living Water's size and overall lack of growth remain the chief factors in its current limitations on how effectively it impacts surrounding communities.

It is certainly not a congregation without its strengths. Although it possesses no clearly defined mission or vision statements in writing, Fountain of Living Water's congregants are unquestionably in agreement when it comes to church goals of reaching out to others in Christlike love and a commitment to spreading the Gospel within the community and beyond. Many of its members regularly participate in local street evangelism ministry. Through its partnership with the Latin America of New York Council, a network of numerous Central New Jersey churches supports missionary efforts throughout Peru and the Dominican Republic. Where there is a known need within the community, whether general poverty or local disaster relief, the congregation pulls together resources to provide individuals and families with food, clothing, and school supplies, though at the time of this writing such mobilization efforts come primarily through the initial efforts of just one congregant.

Fountain of Living Water's pastor is supported by a co-pastor and lay individuals who oversee various small groups organized to administer church functions such as: men's, women's, and children's small groups, missionary support, and fundraising efforts for building purchase. The congregation holds Tuesday night Bible study in addition to its Sunday morning service, which was also held online for a period of time during the COVID-19 shutdown in 2020. Bible study leadership is shared among several congregants, and participants are always encouraged to pursue ministry in light of the Biblical reality that an official title or position is never required in order to be useful in the church.

The congregation's Sunday morning services are held in Spanish, a significant deterrent to attracting non-Spanish speaking visitors, although a volunteer congregant acts as a translator when necessary. There is an overall caring and welcoming atmosphere at Sunday service. The church's diminutive size makes it easier for congregants to get to know one another, to become involved in one another's lives and families, and to foster genuine fellowship and support opportunities. As reasonably expected within a small congregation, Fountain of Living Water enjoys an intimate worship experience where members are encouraged to share a special song or testimony during the service and the benefit of one-on-one prayer afterward, if requested.

Despite its numerous strengths, the church continues to deal with just as many limitations that result primarily from its size and slow growth factors. The lack of diversity among its members and lack of outreach to non-Hispanic members stems primarily from its inability to hold more ministry and community outreach events from a building of its own. A building of its own, the church would also be able to add a second, English-speaking service on Sundays that would feasibly attract more members, particularly those of more diverse groups. With a larger, more diverse congregation come also the opportunities to develop more outreach programs and recruit more volunteer manpower as well as budgetary income to implement those programs. Although it all remains difficult to carry these ideas out without the space and resources required to grow in the first place. It is a Catch-22 dilemma that, as they face the future, continues to plague the faithful within the congregation of Fountain of Living Water.

Summarily, the church faces four immediate priorities:

- ***Development of targeted community outreach*** to not only increase church membership but expand its diversity;
- ***Purchase a church building,*** which will not only provide a congregational meeting space but allow increased opportunity to hold more community events;
- ***Explore developing partnerships with other churches and organizations*** in order to share the financial load of new and existing ministries; and
- ***Increasing an online presence,*** primarily through promotion of the church website and social media engagement for the purpose of spreading the Gospel and keeping local community residents informed about ministry programs and services.

New Horizon Christian Fellowship

New Horizon Christian Fellowship has been a welcoming presence for community members as well as its congregants within

Somerset County, New Jersey for more than 30 years. Though it is a relatively small membership, approximately 45-50 adults and children, it has remained committed to living out the church's core values in light of a "What would Jesus do?" stance, both in members' personal lives as well as the congregation a whole. Despite its many strengths, New Horizon faces ongoing as well as future challenges for maximizing growth and effective community outreach.

In its three decades of existence, New Horizon has never owned its own church building; rather, it holds one Sunday morning service at the school where it rents meeting space and utilizes the same facility for additional church events on an as-needed basis. Like thousands of churches around the world, New Horizon was forced with the task of quickly adjusting to life during the COVID-19 pandemic. When its doors closed for in-person services in the spring of 2020, the church took advantage of opportunities to host a few outdoor services, although it primarily streamed Sunday services online via Facebook and YouTube. Fortunately, its membership remained relatively consistent during the pandemic, and in fact, even gained a few families. New Horizon has maintained a contemporary worship style in its services that effectively blends with a mix of classic hymns, an important factor in impressing the theological and historical richness of traditional forms of worship upon younger congregation members. The church participates in monthly communion and managed to continue the practice even while holding remote services throughout the COVID-19 pandemic.

New Horizon's mission and vision statements are posted on its weekly bulletin as well as the church website, a reflection of their priority and importance within both the congregation as well as its leadership. Due to the modest size of the congregation and the presence of its bi-vocational pastor, lay persons are heavily relied upon to step up and make meaningful contributions in ministry and community outreach whenever possible, including organizing the county's National Day of Prayer each year. Because the church's newer, younger members tend to be just as active in ministry participation as older, established members, it benefits from a good "generational" mix within its regular volunteer force.

Men's and women's Bible studies are held on a weekly basis, and personal discipleship and Bible study are strongly encouraged at New Horizon. Evangelism and missional work are also of high importance, although it has been somewhat difficult to officially sponsor missional programs without a church building. While the church does not specifically budget for missionary support, numerous families within the congregation have personally adopted missionaries that serve across a wide ministry spectrum, including support for missional work focused on rescuing women from sex slavery and prostitution in the U.S. to missions overseas in regions such as Eastern Europe, Turkey, and South America.

With respect to diversity, New Horizon's congregation is comprised of a solid cultural and racial mix, including a few families from Uganda and Nigeria. It does not place special emphasis on creating and building diversity, however, believing instead that congregational diversity comes by God's design rather than a pastor's or anyone else in leadership. Although it recognizes and prays for the contemporary issues and challenges surrounding race relations in the United States, New Horizon chooses to actively focus on the concept of Biblical justice that calls for action to help the needy and poor, whoever that may be, whenever help is needed.

While relatively small and limited in certain capacities, New Horizon is a congregation who enjoys strong Christian fellowship in a close-knit, supportive environment. As of this writing, New Horizon continues working to rebuild the camaraderie of in-person services and meetings among both congregants and newcomers following the COVID-19 pandemic. Summarily, the church faces two priorities for long-term growth and impactful outreach:

- ***Recruit younger members into the congregation to continue the church's work and ministry***, particularly for leadership positions as well as the church board; and
- ***Acquire its own building*** as finances allow, without subtracting time and resources from critical ministries.

St. Martin's Episcopal Church

From its first assembly in 1969 as a gathering of 40 families to more than 210 congregants by 2003, St. Martin's, like many other churches, has seen its share of challenges throughout its 50-year history, including a slight decline in membership that began most notably in 2019.

St. Martin's pastoral leadership has seen a great deal of transition in recent years, a contributing factor to its membership decline. Throughout the transition, however, it has maintained its strong traditional, liturgical sense of worship, communion, and the overall centrality of connectedness among its congregants on

Sunday mornings. A suburban church geographically located near Somerville, New Jersey, St. Martin's is a congregation who remains focused on carrying out the goals surrounding its caring mission and vision statements. This is often reflected in its preaching as well as the many community programs it both sponsors and actively participates in. It operates a school as well as a Montessori daycare, which remained open throughout the entire COVID-19 pandemic, and many of its congregants volunteered with the diocese's food bank and homeless programs within Somerville. Also, St. Martin's upholds a tradition of participating in the Appalachian Service Project, a summer outreach program for teens with a mission to rehabilitate homes for families in need. The congregation does not have an associate pastor but rather relies on the assistance of lay members to carry out the work required in the myriad of outreach programs it oversees.

Statistically speaking, St. Martin's is and has been a congregation composed primarily of white congregants, with few Blacks, Latinos, or Asians. It is a congregation that values and embraces diversity and inclusiveness nevertheless, which is reflected in the anti-racism training and annual interfaith service it participates in through the diocese, as well as the presence of its openly homosexual pastor.

One of the wealthier churches in the region, St. Martin's is a congregation with the financial ability to support ongoing technological advancements, including website development and maintenance, online giving, and virtual church services which were held during the global shutdown, in the early months of the COVID-19 pandemic. Utilizing such tools as a means of greater evangelistic efforts, however, has been another of St. Martin's challenges, even though the church has an evangelism team in place. The general hesitation within its congregation to evangelistically share the Gospel with others outside the church is feasibly another factor contributing to St. Martin's declining membership. The church faces an unknown future continuing into the 21st century and remains a challenge that requires prayerful examination by both its leadership as well as lay members.

Summarily, the church faces two immediate priorities:

- ***Development of targeted community outreach*** to more residents, particularly those of African American, Latino, and Asian descent, with the goal of creating a more diverse congregation; and
- ***Exploration of greater evangelistic efforts*** with the goal of reaching more individuals and families with the Gospel message, including an improved social media and online presence to reach local communities and beyond for Christ.

St. Thomas A.M.E. Zion

When St. Thomas's pastor returned to the congregation in November 2020 after a three-year gap in service, not much had changed within the church during the hiatus. Steeped in rich tradition, St. Thomas A.M.E. remains firmly planted in its age-old existence that revolves deeply around the history of the Somerville, New Jersey community itself. Although today, it also faces the reality of a dwindling existence if it fails to meet certain challenges of the foreseeable future.

Although the congregation boasts of many strengths, its aging membership, coupled with stagnant growth, has become a significant problem for what is known as the oldest Black church in Somerville. It boasts a membership of 75 congregants, with approximately 40% of that membership being most actively involved in church services, worship, and Bible study, while the other 60% seldom participates in ministry activities and tends to fluctuate between attendance at St. Thomas and other local churches. When the COVID-19 pandemic hit and forced churches to close their doors to in-person services, St. Thomas was able to seamlessly transition to holding weekly services via conference call, although a live stream option was eventually added for the benefit of congregants that were more familiar with video technology.

St. Thomas has continued to maintain written vision and mission statements, which it regularly communicates to the congregation at its annual conference as well as publishing them on its weekly service bulletins (a temporary challenge during the COVID-19 pandemic). In the structure of the Methodist tradition, its pastor is supported by lay leadership that assists in overseeing small groups, Sunday school, and Bible study teachings within the church. As a congregation, St. Thomas is committed to meeting the needs of those within the Somerville community and did so during the pandemic. Many congregants actively assisted with local vaccine efforts, operating food kitchens, making hospital visits when possible, and participating in virtual conferences and community awareness initiatives. The overall practice of sharing core values among the membership remains high, although a sense of fellowship is not as strong since the majority of its congregants tend to "church hop" and split membership among other community churches in addition to St. Thomas. As is also in accordance with the Methodist tradition, the church prioritizes global missions, supporting general missionary efforts around the world as well as in-house missionaries within its own congregation.

Significant hindrances to growth and effective community outreach continue to be problematic for St. Thomas. Its opportunities for local missional outreach have become severely restricted simply because of the limited volunteer capacity of its aging membership. Stewardship has also become challenged as many members age and become increasingly reliant upon fixed incomes, although those that do tithe on a regular basis (namely, the 40%) choose to give sacrificially.

Somerville, New Jersey is an overall racially diverse community, although the neighborhoods immediately surrounding St. Thomas are now comprised primarily of white residents. Having existed as a predominantly all-Black church for decades, however, St. Thomas makes little to no effort to diversify its outreach efforts. The potential for new membership to individuals and families are already established in more inclusive churches or congregations closer to their own homes. Ironically, as an African Methodist Episcopal Church, efforts to recruit members of other ethnic or racial groups remain hampered simply in the church name alone. Also, without a younger generation of congregants, St. Thomas is hampered in its outreach efforts to other young Black residents, particularly those that don't identify with the church's history of the Black movement within the community.

Summarily, the church faces several priorities for long-term growth and to maintain its existence:

- ***To continue defining its post-pandemic Sunday worship environment*** by incorporating a hybrid model of church traditions with a "new" worship feel, as the church works to resume in-person services;
- ***To explore ways in which to evangelize the "masses of the unchurched"*** and actively recruit new members, including youth and families and those of other racial and ethnic groups; and
- ***To extend outreach into an online presence,*** including social media and development of a church website.

Trinity United

For many churches, pastoral transition can be a significant challenge that often affects the congregation for months. It was certainly the case at Trinity United when, at the time the COVID-19 pandemic was at its peak in the summer of 2020, the church had not enjoyed the leadership of a permanent pastor for more than three years. As it shifted from in-person to online services during the pandemic shutdown, its newly hired pastor faced the task of shepherding a congregation of members he'd primarily met only in a virtual setting. Trinity continued to broadcast its Sunday morning services via livestream on its website until it resumed in-person services in November 2020.

Since then, however, it has remained relatively strong as a church and has even seen improvement in certain key areas. After the installation of the new pastor in 2020, an internal congregational survey was conducted that ultimately fostered a greater sense of awareness of the church's mission and vision statement among the membership. With a permanent pastor in place, more congregants also became more actively involved in ministry opportunities, including contributions to the local SHARE (Sowing Hope, Reaping Equity) food bank initiative within the Warren, New Jersey community.

Despite the challenges of its pastoral transition in recent years, Trinity has remained a loving, caring, and welcoming environment for visitors as well as its own congregants. Sunday worship services allow members to connect with God's presence through earnest prayer and a blend of traditional hymns along with contemporary songs collected from a variety of sources. Weekly Bible studies are also offered to encourage personal discipleship, although such meetings were also held online during much of the COVID-19 pandemic. The congregation has remained consistently faithful in the area of stewardship, with pledges in 2020 actually exceeding those in the prior year. In the area of missions and community service, Trinity partners with other churches to provide local support on an as-needed basis. The congregation also provides program support for the educational needs of four young girls in Pakistan, although it does not maintain a specific missionary budget for general overseas missions.

Although its small congregation of 38 members did not decrease as a result of the COVID-19 pandemic, Trinity's growth has stunted, as it has for many other churches in the U.S. in recent years. Its membership, comprised of mostly White, middle-aged congregants, also lacks a significant level of diversity in racial, ethnic, and age composition and the church is exploring ways on how to reach out not only to individuals of varying backgrounds but to become a more inviting presence to more youth and families.

Summarily, the church currently faces two priorities for long-term growth:

- ***To increase outreach to a more diverse population and develop a meaningful presence within the community,*** including the recruitment of external volunteers to help implement greater support and ministry outreach through programs such as the SHARE food distribution initiative; and
- ***Explore ways to expand outreach through the church's existing technological means,*** including its social media presence and use of its website.

As we come to the end of this project by reflecting on the challenges and successes of these profiled congregations, we must remember that this is not the end but simply a continuation. This is a great opportunity for new beginnings. New things, situations, and opportunities that is always exciting. They represent the chance to do something different in anticipation of a fresh start. Something new isn't always appealing, but when it comes to our walk of faith, "new" is always important because God himself is always up to something new. We may not understand all the pieces of the puzzle he's putting together, but we know that the whole will always be undeniably good because *he* is good.

Although past experiences can help us look forward to the future with hope, dwelling too much on the past can hinder us from following God into the new things that he will do in the future. One of the greatest reminders of this in scripture can be found in Isaiah 43, when many Jews had been taken into exile and were suffering under Babylonian rule. The people were feeling the physical, economic, cultural, and religious oppression of Babylon. One of the prophet Isaiah's tasks was to rebuild the people's understanding of themselves as God's own people. To reassure them that their God was entirely capable of taking on the Babylonian superpower in order to save them. In a seemingly hopeless situation, Isaiah called on the people not to lose heart but to look with anticipation for the signs of God's approaching redemption, for the "new thing" that is coming:

> This is what the Lord says—he who made a way through the sea, a path through the mighty waters, who drew out the chariots and horses, the army and reinforcements together, and they lay there, never to rise again, extinguished, snuffed out like a wick: "Forget the former things; do not dwell on the past. See, I am doing a new thing! Now it springs up; do you not perceive it? I am making a way in the wilderness and streams in the wasteland. (Isaiah 43:16-19)

With further, careful study of these passages, we can conclude that Isaiah was encouraging God's people to do three things:

1. ***Remember not the former things of the past;***
2. ***Be open to God's new thing; and***
3. ***Remember that God is in the process of bringing a new thing into reality.***

In clarification of these three points, it is not in the past that the prophet Isaiah wanted the people to concentrate on. It was rather their ability to create an imaginative space in their minds so that their conception of the past could transform their understanding of the present, and thus, the future. If we were to apply this to our own lives and personal walk-in faith, it could be said that God's call for us to prepare for a new thing. This reminds us that it is God who, in his redemptive grace, comes in his holiness to make each of us whole. And that he can fashion whatever he wants to in us regardless of the circumstances we may face or current events in the world.

Now what, you may be asking, what does this concept of "doing a new thing" have to do with church health and faithfulness? Everything, as a matter of fact. Simply put, the church should not be so resistant to change that it overlooks the blessed opportunity to participate in God's "new thing," and how he is choosing to use his church in the world for his purposes on this side of eternity. What's more, it can also be said that, when a congregation resolves to examine its own vitality through the consideration of health and faithfulness factors, it is not just looking at the situation in the present time, it is trusting God in the anticipation of and planning for a "new thing," a better future, and prayerfully considering how that future can more effectively impact others for Christ.

With these thoughts regarding "a new thing" in mind, it is only fitting to end this chapter, and ultimately this book, with insights regarding church health and faithfulness from the pastor of Liquid Church, a newly established (at the time of this writing) congregation in Somerville, New Jersey:

Interview with Pastor Jon, Liquid Church (One Church)

1. **Please describe in detail your calling and journey to start a new church plant.**

   As a young man, I accepted Jesus as my personal Lord and Savior through the investment and mentorship of my parents and grandfather, who served as lead pastor of our church. So, I grew up watching my grandfather preach every week thinking, "that's what I want to do!"

   I had an opportunity to help plant a church right out of college where I oversaw the worship experience and sat on the leadership team for the church. It was such a great experience for over a year, but then a culture of toxicity set in on the leadership team that was made up entirely of a family with the lead pastor and his wife as well as his sister. The church didn't grow as they expected and finger pointing started to happen; the net result for me was that my wife and I left, wounded by the church we loved.

   It would be several years before my wife and I began to feel comfortable in any kind of church leadership again. I started with volunteering at Liquid Church and slowly worked into leadership and ultimately two pastoral roles; first as an associate pastor in 2014 and then as the planting campus pastor for the newest location in 2015. (In the Liquid/multisite world, campuses are churches in different locations that share the same DNA as the rest of the church.

They launch new campuses, primarily with video teaching, to reach a broader audience. I oversaw and led one of their campuses.)

It was just about a year into my role as campus pastor that God began to stir in me that there was more for me. I was really starting to struggle with the organizational, matrix structure of a multisite church that focuses control centrally. There were things that I felt God was placing on my heart that I couldn't really lean into in my current role because there was a larger, central organization making decisions globally and I always needed to be mindful of that. I also had a desire to preach and there was very little opportunity to lean into that. God had placed this burning in my spirit to share his Word but, as a part of a church that uses video as the primary source of teaching, I didn't have opportunity to do that.

I was at a crossroads where I felt I either needed to leave the church I was at or find some sense of relief because it was starting to hurt my soul. So, in January of 2017, I fasted for 21 days and towards the end of the fast God spoke directly to my spirit. He told me that He was affirming in me all the desires and gifts that He had placed in me…but, he needed me to be patient and wait. His timing is perfect and I still had much to learn.

So, I waited for several years before God made it clear that He was asking me to plant a new church. I was being recruited to and looked into joining a few other churches in 2020 to launch a campus, take over leadership for a campus, or become a lead pastor at a local church. Each had its own appeal and I certainly explored each opportunity, but I never felt peace in any of the situations. That's when God really placed it on my heart and made it crystal clear that he wanted me to plant a church.

There was a decisive moment for us when my wife and I both sensed that God was parting the Jordan River so we could enter the promised land He had for us. In March of 2021, my leadership at Liquid Church had come to me with the unanimous decision that they were going to close my 600+ person campus (church) and wanted me to move it an hour south to a new location. It felt so obvious to us that this was the right time because Somerville is where God was calling me to be and now my church was gone. I believed that God could use me to fill the void that was left as I answered His calling to start a new church.

As with all decisions, the decision to plant a church should never be made lightly. There were three key aspects of the decision that I looked at to determine if this was truly what God was calling me to do. I had to start here and process these questions before I could take the next step. Otherwise, the decision could very well simply be my decision, based on my ambition and talent, without the support and direction of the Holy Spirit. I needed to know that God was in this.

The first question I needed an answer to was, is this idea backed up in scripture? Well, the entirety of the Book of Acts is the story of the early church coming into existence and growing with new churches planting everywhere. That, considering the Great Commission to "go and make disciples", I felt convinced that the decision to start a new church was certainly backed up in scripture.

The second question I needed to answer was whether or not I had sought wise counsel and what insights did that counsel provide? So, before making the final decision I sought advice and feedback from a multitude of counselors including trusted friends and family, other local pastors that I have relationships with and trusted for honest feedback, and other ministry relationships that I have journeyed with along the way. The resounding feedback was of excitement and joy. The common thread in the feedback was that this is good and right. So, I felt convinced that I had received wise counsel from trusted, Godly sources and that the response was in the affirmative toward planting.

The third question I needed answered was whether God had granted peace over this. Thankfully, after much prayer and petition with my wife, God had granted each of us peace over this decision and confirmation that the timing was now. We had not jointly felt peace prior to that moment, but God had now intervened and made it clear that this was right.

In 2021, I started to write down the vision and values that God was placing on my heart, left Liquid Church, and planted One Church.

2. **What is the vision, mission and core values and ministries of One Church?**

The vision of One Church is "To be ONE in Christ by embracing the irresistible grace of Jesus." We have a vision of unity that comes from Jesus' prayer in John 17:21 (NLT) where he prays "I pray that they will all be one, just as you and I are one—as you are in me, Father, and I am in you. And may they be in us so that the world will believe you sent me." We believe that the best way that we can represent Jesus to the world around us is by coming together in love, despite our differences.

The mission statement for One Church is "To create a community of believers dedicated to living in unity by loving and serving others and getting proximate to our local community." It's a mission of oneness and community. We will live in unity with one another, loving and serving each other and helping each other to grow in our faith, as we get proximate to the greater community around us. We will be involved and will be known for our generosity and community outreach.

Finally, the Core Values of One Church are:

Unity - Jesus prays for his church to be unified. So, we hold fast to what makes us Christian, as represented in our statement of beliefs, and loosen our grip on the nonessentials that tend to drive us apart. We can come together as a community, in a safe environment, to explore God's word and apply it to our lives. John 17:21, 1 Corinthians 1:10-17, Ephesians 4:1-14

Diversity - Part of the role of the believer and the church is to usher in the Kingdom of God on Earth as it is in Heaven. Part of our responsibility and the way we do that is to have our community reflect what the Kingdom of God actually looks like. That means we will be intentional to reflect and value every nation, tribe, people, and language. Matthew 6:10, Revelations 7:9, James 2:1-9, Ephesians 2:11-22

Simplicity - In many ways the "Church" has complicated faith and what it means to be a Christian or what it means to be a church. We think church should be simple, so we will invest far more in our community and the community around us than we will in our services and production. We will not do anything for self-promotion and make a commitment to humility, recognizing that our goal as a church is never about numbers, power and influence, but instead about true conversion and lives changed. Great leaders serve! Acts 2:42-47

Generosity - We will be known by how generous we are in giving of our time, talents and resources. As we practice simple church principles we will give generously to our community both inside and outside the church. Acts 2:42-47 James 1:27

Community - The early church devoted themselves to fellowship, caring for each other and being together. To do this they understood that grace is the defining aspect of our faith. God extends his grace to each of us so we must lead with grace in our relationships with one another. The quality and depth of our relationships and our testimony of grace will be defined by how we love and serve one another. This love of community will be counter cultural to the world around us as the gospel is counter-cultural to the world around us. Acts 2:42-47, Hebrews 10:24-25

Participation - God has empowered and gifted each of us in different ways and with different talents and abilities. The expectation is that we use what he has given for the glory of God and the growth of his Kingdom. We will be action minded and will be known by how we participate in God's vision through teams, outreaches and small groups. Acts 2:42-47, 1 Corinthians 12:20-26

Authenticity - Authenticity is a calling of all believers. We will let our yes be yes and our no be no. We will be honest, transparent and authentic in all we say and do. We will be prepared and ready to have the hard conversations, in love, with grace and truth, and are willing to have those conversations without needing to have all the answers. James 5:12, Romans 12:9, 1 Corinthians 2:1-5

Multiplication - Our goal is not to become a megachurch but to grow deeper into community and relationships. Because of this, we believe the best way to grow the kingdom is by multiplying the church. We will continue to send people from our community, with resources, encouragement and prayer, to plant new churches wherever God calls them to do it. Matthew 24:14, Matthew 28:19, 1 Corinthians 3:7, 1 Corinthians 12:20-26

3. **What is God calling One Church to be in the life of the community and world?**

As with all churches, our calling is to be the light of the world around us. We are to share the love of Christ and reach people with his Gospel truth. However, as summed up in our vision and mission, we believe that the best way to do this is by living in unity with each other within our church as well as with those outside and in other churches. We want people to see Jesus so clearly by the way we love one another.

4. **What changes, if any, do you foresee happening in the next 3-5 years?**

Over the next 3-5 years I believe there will be a movement back to authentic worship of God. I believe that people will begin to grow tired of the show that so many churches feel they need to put on in order to reach people, and they are going to want to learn more Biblical truth and to have an encounter with the Holy Spirit.

In light of that, I think churches will move away from the megachurch model and move into more of a multiplication model for growth. The community will become more and more of a focus especially as we come out of a pandemic season of isolation.

I also think that having a digital footprint will continue to become more and more essential to reaching new people. Websites, social media, and platforms like YouTube will continue to drive engagement, especially with respect to being the front door of the church. Most people want to know what to expect before they come in so having excellent online communications will help to relay the culture that exists at the church. However, while there was a massive push to online church during the pandemic, I believe that we will see a correction as people will seek to gather together in person more than has happened in many years.

Along those same lines, I believe that small groups will also continue to grow in strength over the next 3-5 years. People want community and discipleship (even if they don't use that word) and those things can't be restricted to just Sunday worship. While important, "church" must happen outside the walls of the church building as people come together to break bread, worship, study and care for one another's needs.

5. **Please share your insights with others who may be contemplating starting a new church. Please identify the health and faithfulness factors you feel are most important in starting a new church plant.**

Starting a new church has been the single greatest joy of my ministry life thus far! However, I do not believe that it is for everyone. You need an entrepreneurial spirit and drive to move it forward. It takes a lot of hours and a lot of hard work as you work to get everything set up, meet people and prepare for services. It is exhausting but exhilarating if you are called to do it. If you are not called, it will just be exhausting. Here are a few of my insights as they pertain to health and faithfulness in church planting:

- Make sure this is what God is actually calling you to do.
- Consult with wise counsel in your life. Ask them to be honest with you about whether this is the right time.
- Don't move forward without peace. If God is not in this with you then it can tear you apart. Seek him and don't move forward unless he has granted you peace.
- Focus more on the people than the process. Build a core team that will be invested in

you and what God is calling you to do. Build those relationships and get their buy-in. You will need their expertise, time, talents, and resources to pull this off. The tendency is to focus on the thing as what will draw people in. The truth is that people want a relationship with their leader so meet them there first.

- Create a vision that lines up with scripture and encourages people to be involved. People will always give of their time, talents, and resources, to vision way more than to things. Sell the vision before you ask for your needs. Discover and write down what God is speaking to you, and what you are getting excited about and share that with others. If people buy into the vision they will take care of your needs.
- Develop healthy rhythms of rest and restoration. This has been the hardest one for me because there is just so much to do. However, you cannot lead people into healthy rhythms if you aren't healthy yourself. You can't lead people into a restorative relationship with Jesus if you are being restored yourself. You need to be in the Word yourself. You need to be in constant prayer yourself. You need to be discipled if you are going to disciple others.

Don't focus so much on doing for Jesus that you neglect being with Jesus.

- Don't forget to just sit in wonder at the majesty of God Almighty. We get to be his representation here on earth. We get to be his hands and feet and introduce people to him. Don't lose that sense of wonder in what God can do in and through you. If God calls you into this and gives you vision he will also give you the provision. Rest in that and sit in awe that God Almighty would use you to grow and build His Kingdom here on earth as it is in heaven.

While the birth of Liquid Church is a terrific example of congregational vision that began many years ago in Pastor Jon's life and heart, the overall notion of a "new thing" has never been more prevalent in the history of the church than now when, at the time of this writing, the world and many church doors are re-opening following the worst of the COVID-19 pandemic. In light of this, among other global and societal changes already examined throughout this book, another crucial question remains: is God, indeed, doing a new thing today? Just as importantly, another question for reflection is, how will we respond to his new thing, and as his church, will we be open to accepting the new things that God is doing?

In summary, each member of the body of Christ must be prepared to ask themselves and honestly answer those questions.

Uncovering the answers to those questions, one leader, one member, one congregation at a time has remained the goal of this health and faithfulness project. Now, the challenge rests on you, the reader: how will *you* go forth from here? How will you advocate for necessary change and support, to ***re-think***, ***re-engage***, and ***reimagine***, within your own congregation, your own community, for the sake of Christ's Gospel?

Let the challenge continue.

Questions for Reflection

1. What similarities did you notice about each of the six congregations? What differences?

2. As you consider the strengths and weaknesses of your own congregation, what are the most notable changes you have observed over the past two years? One year?

3. After reading about this congregational health and faithfulness project, are you more inclined to share these findings with your own church leadership or congregation? Why or why not?

Appendix A

Church Health Questionnaire

Categories	Clarity of Mission and/ or Vision	Authentic Worship	Pastoral and Church leadership	Discipleship	Caring and Loving Fellowship	Core Values
A Sense of Urgency ***(1)*** **(Members are greatly concerned and immediate attention is needed.)**	Very few members know the mission and/or vision statement.	Members do not experience the presence of God and have their spiritual needs met. (prayer, music, preached word, i.e.)	Very few members are involved in the mission and ministry of the church.	Members are not actively involved in learning and growing in God's word.	People and members do not feel a sense of belonging to the church.	Members do not demonstrate harmony, unity, fellowship and love in the church
Needs Attention ***(2)*** **(We have concern and it needs attention)**	Members know about the mission/vision statement but are weak on action.	Very few members connect with the church services (order, prayer, music style, length of service, i.e.)	Members are seldom involved in the mission and ministry of the church.	Very few members are actively involved in learning and growing in God's word. (Attend Sunday school, Bible study and other Christian education activities).	People and members have a limited sense of belonging to the church.	Members seldom demonstrate very little harmony, unity, fellowship and love in the church.

Good *(3)* **(We are average, nothing exceptional, and no real concern).**	Members know about the mission/vision statement and make some efforts to follow through on implementation	Members connect with the spiritual presence of God.	Members are encouraged to become actively involved in the church's mission and ministry.	Members are encouraged to become actively involved in learning and growing in God's Word (attend Sunday school, Bible study, Christian education activities).	People and members have a sense of belonging to the church.	Members demonstrate harmony, unity, fellowship and love in the church.
Very Good *(4)* **(We have made some progress).**	Members know about the mission/vision statement and are motivated to follow through on the implementation	Members connect with the presence of God and have their spiritual needs fulfilled.	Members are encouraged by the pastor to become actively involved in the church's mission and ministry.	Members are encouraged by the pastor to become more involved in learning and growing in God's word.	People, members and Church leaders have a greater sense of belonging to the church.	Members are encouraged by the pastor to demonstration harmony, unity, fellowship and love in the church
Exceptional *(5)* **(We have made great progress in working toward our mission and vision goals).**	Members know about the mission/vision statement and monitor their progress toward implementation	The majority of the members connect with the presence of God and have their spiritual needs fulfilled.	Members are encouraged by the pastor and church leaders to become actively involved in the church's mission and ministry.	Members are encouraged by the pastor and church leaders to become more involved in the learning and growing of God's word.	People and members have a sense of belonging to the church and are nurtured by the pastor and church leaders.	Members are encouraged by pastors and leaders to demonstrate harmony, unity, fellowship and love in the church
Score						

Appendix B

Church Faithfulness Questionnaire

Categories	Evangelism and Missional Outreach	Stewardship	Outward Community Focus	Cultural and Racial Diversity	Social Advocacy, and Networking	Missions (Global, National, State, and Local)
A Sense of Urgency *(1)* **(Members are greatly concerned and immediate attention is needed.)**	No invitation is ex-tended by members to share and wittiness to the gospel of Jesus Christ with others in the community.	Members give very little of time, talents and financial resources to support church programs, activities and ministries.	The church scheduling ministries, events and activities for members within the church.	Cultural and racial diversity is nonexistent in the church leadership and membership.	There is no active engagement by the church to network, advocate and mobilize resources to address inequality, social injustices, and poverty in the community.	There are no mission opportunities for the church to demonstrate the love of Christ by serving people in need globally, nationally and locally.
Needs Attention *(2)* **(We have concern and it needs attention)**	An occasional invitation by members to share and witness to the gospel of Jesus Christ with others in the community	Members give as needed their time, talents and financial resources to support church programs, activities and ministries.	The church scheduling ministries, events and activities without input from community residents.	Cultural and racial diversity is not a major priority in the existing church leadership and membership.	There is limited active engagement by the church to network, advocate, and mobilize resources to address inequality, social justices, and poverty in the community.	There are few mission opportunities for the church to demonstrate the love of Christ by serving people in need globally, nationally and locally.

Good *(3)* **(We are average, nothing exceptional, and no real concern).**	An open invitation is extended by members to share and witness to the gospel of Jesus Christ with others in the community	Members give regularly their time, talents, and financial resources to support the church programs, activities, and ministries	The church scheduling ministries, events and activities with input from community residents.	Cultural and racial diversity is a priority within the church leadership and membership	There is active engagement by the church to network, advocate, and mobilize resources to address the issues of inequality, social injustices, and poverty in the community.	There are mission opportunities that the church participates and demonstrate the love of Christ in need globally, nationally and locally.
Very Good *(4)* **(We have made some progress).**	An intentional invitation is extended by members and church leaders to share and witness to the gospel of Jesus Christ with others in the community.	Members and church leaders give on a regular basis time, talents and financial resources to support church programs, activities and ministries.	Members and church leaders are intentional about scheduling ministries, events and activities for reaching the community.	Members and church leaders are intentional about working toward cultural and racial diversity within the church membership.	There is active engagement by the members and Church leaders to network, advocate and mobilize resources to address the issues of inequality, social injustices and poverty in the community.	There are intentional mission opportunities the church actively supports, participate and demonstrates the love of Christ by serving people in need globally, nationally and locally.

Exceptional (5) **(We have made great progress in working toward our mission and vision goals).**	An intentional invitation and follow up is extended by members, church leaders, and the pastor to share and witness to the gospel of Jesus with others in the community	Members, church leaders, and pastor give beyond what is required of time, talents and financial resources to support church programs, activities and ministries.	Members, church leaders and church pastor are intentional about scheduling ministries, events and activities for reaching and addressing the needs of the community.	Members, church leaders and pastor are intentional about working toward cultural and racial diversity within the church programs, ministries, and activities.	There is active engagement by the pastor, leaders, and membership to network, advocate, and mobilize resources to address the issues of inequality, social injustices and poverty in the community.	There are intentional mission opportunities that the pastor, leaders, and membership support and participate regularly and demonstrate the love of Christ by serving people in need globally, nationally and locally.
Score						

Appendix C

Community Assets Map

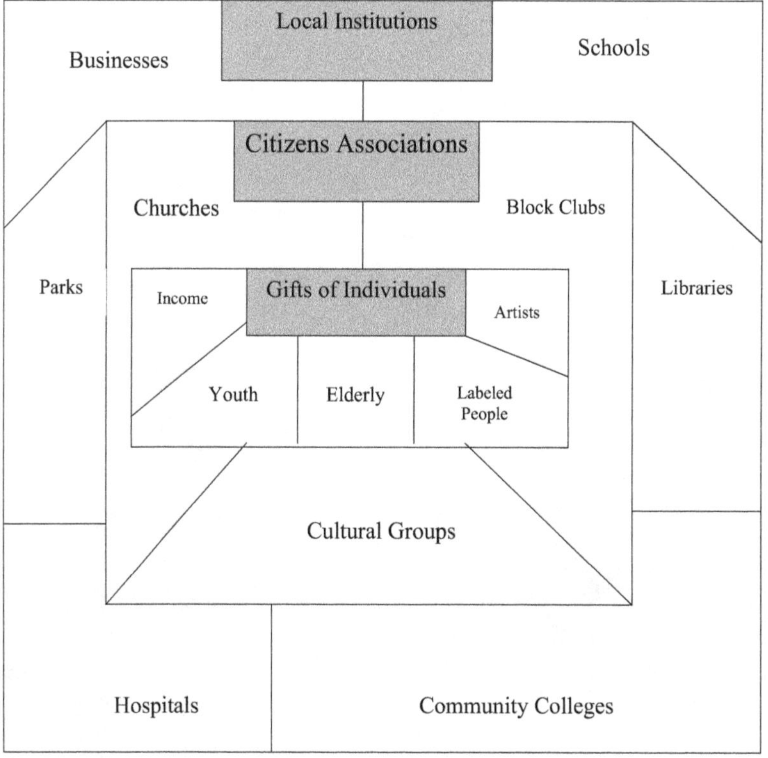

Bibliography

Books

Barna, George, and Navigators. 1993. *Marketing the Church.* Colorado Springs, Colo.: Navpress.

Bonhoeffer, Dietrich, "Life Together," in *Dietrich Bonhoeffer Works,* ed. Geffrey B. Kelley, trans. Daniel W. Bloesch and James H. Burtness (Minneapolis: Fortress, 1996).

Callahan, L. Kennon, *Twelve Keys to an Effective Church: Strong, Healthy Congregations Living in the Grace of God*: Jossey- Bass: San Francisco, California, 2nd Edition: 2009.

Carroll W. Jackson, Dudley, S. Carl, and McKinney William, *Handbook for Congregational Studies*: Nashville: Abingdon Press:1987.

Engen, Van Charles, *God's Missionary People: Rethinking the Purpose of the Local Church* (Grand Rapids, Michigan: Baker Books, 1991).

Gelder, Van Craig, *The Essence of the Church: A Community Created by the Spirit* (Grand Rapids, Michigan: Baker Books, 2000.

Gelder, Van Craig, *The Ministry of the Missional Church: A Community Led By The Spirit* (Grand Rapids, Michigan: Baker Books, 2007).

Hilliard, Donald, *Church Growth from An African American Perspective,* (Judson Press: Valley Forge Pennsylvania, 2006).

Hiscox T. Edward, *The Hiscox Standard Baptist Manual* (Valley Forge, Pennsylvania: Judson Press, 1965).

Kretzmann P. John, Mcknight, L. John, *Building Communities from the Inside Out: A Path Toward Finding and Mobilizing a Community's Assets*, Evanston, Illinois: Institute for Policy Research, 1993.

Macchia, Stephen, *Becoming A Healthy Church: Ten Traits of A Vital Ministry*: Baker Books: Grand Rapids: Michigan, 1999.

Malphurs, Aubrey, *A New Kind of Church: Understanding Models of Ministry for the 21st Century* (Grand Rapids, Michigan: Baker Books, 2007).

Malphurs Aubrey, *Strategic Disciple Making: A Practical Tool for Successful Ministry* (Grand Rapids, Michigan: Baker Books Publishing, 2009.

Mann Alice, *Can Our Church Live: Redeveloping Congregations in Decline,* Bethesda, Maryland: Alban Institute, 1999.

McGavran, Donald, *Bridges of God: A Study in the Strategy of Missions,* Wipf and Stock Publishers: Eugene, Oregon, 2005.

McGavran, Donald, *Understanding Church Growth*: Grand Rapids, Michigan, 1970.

Miller, Keith, *The Taste of New Wine,* Formation Press: Austin Texas, 2009 (Third Revised Edition).

Newbigin, Lesslie, *The Open Secret: An Introduction to the Theology of Mission* (Grand Rapids, Michigan: Eerdmans, 1995).

Quinn, E. Robert, *Deep Change: Discovering the Leader Within,* San Francisco, California: Jossey-Bass, 1996.

Schwarz, Christian, *Natural Church Development: A Guide to Eight Essential Qualities of Healthy Churches.* Inter Ctr for Leadership Dev. &, 1996.

Senge, Peter M. *The Fifth Discipline: The Art and Practice of the Learning Organization,* New York Doubleday/Currency, 1990.

Snyder A. Howard, The *Community of the King,* Downers Grove, Illinois: Inter-Varsity, 1977.

Spitzer. Lee, *Endless Possibilities* Course Book Spiral-bound, Spiritual Journey Press: Bordentown, New Jersey 1997.

Stedman, Ray, *Body Life: The Book That Inspired a Return to the Church's Real Meaning and Mission*: Discovery House Publishers: Grand Rapids Michigan, 1995.

Warren, Rick, *The Purpose Driven Church,* Zondervan: Grand Rapids: Michigan., 1995.

Website Articles

Hertig, Paul. 2001. "The Great Commission Revisited: The Role of God's Reign in Disciple Making." *Missiology: An International Review* 29 (3): 343–53. https://doi.org/10.1177/009182960102900306.

Rainer, S. Thom, "Shattering Myths about the Un-churched," *Southern Baptist Journal of Theology 5,* no. 1 (Spring 2001): 47.

Gil, Rendle, "Twelve Characteristics for Effective 21st-Century Ministry," https://alban.org › archive. Alban Institute, July 24, 2006.

Shepson Bill, "Who are the Unchurched?" *The Foursquare Church.* http://www.foursquare.org/news/article/who_are_theunchurched, (accessed March 25, 2011).

Spencer, James. n.d. Spencer, James, http://www.nextgenchristians.com, https://Nextgenchristians.com/2020/05/26/Inertia-Confronting-Our-Tendency-To-Continue-Unchanged/, May 26, 2020.

"The Millennial's Guide to the Older Generations," 2015. March 3, 2015. https://www.pts.edu/blog/author/ptsblog.

"Connecting the Generations CT Pastors." n.d. Www.christianitytoday.com. Accessed August 15, 2022. https://christianitytoday.com/pastors/channel/utilities/print.html?type=article&id=9722.

"FALLING through the NET: A Survey of the 'Have Nots' in Rural and Urban America | National Telecommunications and Information Administration." 2019. Doc.gov. 2019. https://www.ntia.doc.gov/ntiahome/fallingthru.html.

"National Black Church Initiative - Digital Divide Initiative." n.d. Www.naltblackchurch.com. Accessed August 15, 2022. https://www.naltblackchurch.com/technology/.

Magazine, Outreach. 2020. "Digital-Savvy Churches See Consistent Giving during Pandemic." OutreachMagazine.com. July 15, 2020. https://outreachmagazine.com/resources/research-and-trends/57523-digital-savvy-churches-see-consistent-giving-during-pandemic.html.

Research, Lifeway. 2011. "Churches Divided on Web Use." Lifeway Research. January 21, 2011. https://lifewayresearch.com/2011/01/21/lifeway-research-finds-churches-divided-on-web-use/.

"White Christians Have Become Even Less Motivated to Address Racial Injustice." n.d. Barna Group. https://www.barna.com/research/american-christians-race-problem/.

"Multiracial Congregations May Not Bridge Racial Divide." n.d. NPR.org. https://www.npr.org/2020/07/17/891600067/multiracial-congregations-may-not-bridge-racial-divide.

"Common Ground, Hard Truths & next Steps: A Panel on Racial Justice." 2020. Barna Group. June 2, 2020. https://www.barna.com/racial-justice-panel/.

"WhatAmericansThinkaboutWomeninPower."n.d.BarnaGroup.https://www.barna.com/research/americans-think-women-power/.

"CBE's Mission and Values." n.d. CBE International. https://www.cbeinternational.org/content/cbes-mission.

"Are Some Complementarian Practices Gaslighting?" 2019. The Art of Taleh. October 17, 2019. https://www.theartoftaleh.com/are-some-complementarian-practices-gaslighting/.

West, Steven D. 2022. "Christian Ethics." The Gospel Coalition. 2022. https://www.thegospelcoalition.org/essay/christian-ethics/.

Gilson, Tom. 2018. "Handling Ethical Issues: Five Reasons Your Church ProbablyIsn'tTeachingEnoughonIt."TheStream.July21,2018.https://stream.org/hot-ethical-issues-five-reasons-church-teaching/.

West, Steven D. 2022. "Christian Ethics." The Gospel Coalition. 2022. https://www.thegospelcoalition.org/essay/christian-ethics/.

"Pastors Prefer Lay-Led Initiatives to New Church Programs but Struggle to Develop Leaders." n.d. Barna Group. Accessed August 15, 2022. https://www.barna.com/research/inspire-people-to-action/.

"StackPath." n.d. Leadnet.org. Accessed August 15, 2022. https://leadnet.org/10-truths-of-churches-that-do-a-great-job-with-leadership-development-part-2/.

"Church Planning Part 2: Elements of a Strategic Plan | OnStrategy Resources." n.d. Onstrategyhq.com. https://onstrategyhq.com/resources/church-planning-part-2-elements-of-a-strategic-plan/.

Endnotes

1 "Barna Describes Religious Changes Among Busters, Boomers, and Elders Since 1991," https://www.barna.com/research/barna-describes-religious-changes-among-busters-boomers-and-elders-since-1991/, July 26, 2011.

2 "U.S. Church Membership Falls Below Majority for First Time," Jones, Jeffrey M., Mar. 21, 2021, https://news.gallup.com/poll/341963/church-membership-falls-below-majority-first-time.aspx

3 "3 Characteristics of an Effective Purpose Statement." Accessed April 13, 2022. https://pastors.com/3-characteristics-of-an-effective-purpose-statement/.

4 https://www.microsoft.com/en-us/about.

5 Senge, Peter M. *The Fifth Discipline: The Art and Practice of the Learning Organization*, New York Doubleday/Currency, 1990, p. 4.

6 Irwin, Travis. "Core Values & Your Church," https://churchinvolvement.com/2016/05/core-values-your-church/, May 5, 2016.

7 "May 2016 – Church Involvement," accessed April 13, 2022, https://churchinvolvement.com/2016/05/.

8 "Twelve Characteristics for Effective 21st-Century Ministry," accessed April 13, 2022, https://alban.org/archive/twelve-characteristics-for-effective-21st-century-ministry/.

9 Greek: διακονία, diakonia (G1248) - Bible - Quotes Cosmos https://www.quotescosmos.com >Strong's Bible-concordance.

10 Carroll W. Jackson, Dudley, S. Carl, and McKinney William, *Handbook for Congregational Studies*: Nashville: Abingdon Press: 1987, pp. 49-50.

11 *Ibid.*, pp. 21-24.

12 *Ibid.*, pp. 120-124.

13 https://studybible.info/vines/Worship%20(Verb%20and%20Noun),%20 Worshiping.

14 Somerset County Library System of New Jersey: Complete Community Demographics Summary Report of Somerset Townships, Gale Company: Accessed June 3, 2021.

15 Ronald Carlson, Dr., "Definition of the Missional Church," National Ministries, American Baptist Churches USA, 2007. http://www.nationalministries.org. (accessed November 28, 2021).

16 Howard A. Snyder, *The Community of the King* (Downers Grove, Illinois: Inter-Varsity, 1977), 117-118.

17 *Ibid.*,125-126.

18 Pentecostal/Charismatic Movement | Timeline -https://www.thearda.com › movements › movement_42, https://thearda.com/timeline/movements/movement_42.asp.

19 https://www.compellingtruth.org/charis-in-the-Bible.html.

20 C. Peter Wager and Donald A, McGavran, *Understanding Church Growth*, Wm B. Eerdmans Publishing Co. pp. 70-71, 1970.

21 "Donald McGavran and the Church Growth Movement," Helwys Society Forum, http://www.helwyssocietyforum.com/donald-mcgavran-and-the-church-growth-movement/, Feb. 3, 2014.

22 Donald Anderson McGavran, *The Bridges of God: A Study in the Strategy of Missions*: Wipf and Stock Publishers: 2005. pp. 13-15.

23 Gary L. Mclintosh, "Church Movements of the Last Fifty Years in the USA," March 13, p.3, 2015. https://www.churchgrowthnetwork.com'

24 Donald Hilliard Jr., *Church Growth from an African American Perspective* (Valley Forge, Pennsylvania: Judson Press), p. 10.

25 Arthur, Eddie, "Missio Dei and the Mission of the Church," Accessed August 19, 2019, https://www.wycliffe.net/more-about-what-we-do/papers-and-articles/missio-dei-and-the-mission-of-the-church/.

26 Charles Van Engen, *God's Missionary People: Rethinking the Purpose of the Local Church* (Grand Rapids, Michigan: Baker Books, 1991), 35-36.

27 Craig Van Gelder, *The Ministry of the Missional Church: A Community Led By The Spirit* (Grand Rapids, Michigan: Baker Books, 2007), 54-55.

28 Craig Van Gelder, *The Essence of the Church: A Community Created by the Spirit* (Grand Rapids, Michigan: Baker Books, 2000) p. 37.

29 *Ibid.*, 32.

30 Paul Hertig, "The Great Commission Revisited: The Role of God's Reign in Disciple Making," *Missiology: An International Review* 29. no.3 (July 2001), 348.

31 Aubrey Malphurs, *Strategic Disciple Making: A Practical Tool for Successful Ministry* (Grand Rapids, Michigan: Baker Books Publishing, 2009), 19.

32 *Ibid.*

33 *Ibid.*

34 Donald Hilliard Jr., *Church Growth from an African American Perspective* (Valley Forge, Pennsylvania: Judson Press), 4.

35 *Ibid.*, 12

36 Edward T. Hiscox, *The Hiscox Standard Baptist Manual* (Valley Forge, Pennsylvania: Judson Press, 1965), 10-11.

37 Craig Van Gelder, *The Essence of the Church: A Community Created by the Spirit* (Grand Rapids, Michigan: Baker Books, 2000), 74.

38 *Ibid.*

39 Lesslie Newbigin, *The Open Secret: An Introduction to the Theology of Mission* (Grand Rapids, Michigan: Eerdmans, 1995), 30-31.

40 Dietrich Bonhoeffer, "Life Together," in *Dietrich Bonhoeffer Works*, ed. Geffrey B. Kelley, trans. Daniel W. Bloesch and James H. Burtness (Minneapolis: Fortress, 1996), 5:33.

41 Hilliard, *Church Growth from an African American Perspective*, 13.

42 Robert E. Quinn, *Deep Change: Discovering the Leader Within* (San Francisco, California: Jossey-Bass, 1996), 159.

43 Alice Mann, *Can Our Church Live: Redeveloping Congregations in Decline* (Bethesda, Maryland: Alban Institute, 1999), 2.

44 *Ibid.*, 1.

45 *Ibid.*, 5.

46 *Ibid.*, 5.

47 *Ibid*, 7.

48 *Ibid.*, 8.

49 https://www.who.int › About WHO › Governance

50 Spencer, James, http://www.nextgenchristians.com, https://nextgenchristians.com/2020/05/26/inertia-confronting-our-tendency-to-continue-unchanged/, May 26, 2020.

51 "The Millennial's Guide to the Older Generations," https://www.pts.edu/blog/author/ptsblog, March 3, 2015.

52 Zahn, Drew, "Connecting the Generations," Christianity Today, https://christianitytoday.com/pastors/channel/utilities/print.html?type=article&id=9722, April 1, 2002.

53 U.S. Department of Commerce, National Telecommunications and Information Administration (NTIA). (1995). Falling through the net: A survey of the have nots in rural and urban America. Retrieved from, http://www.ntia.doc.gov/ntiahome/fallingthru.html.

54 National Black Church Initiative, https://www.naltblackchurch.com/technology/.

55 "Digital Savvy Churches See Consistent Giving During Pandemic," Outreach Magazine, July 15, 2020, https://outreachmagazine.com/resources/research-and-trends/57523-digital-savvy-churches-see-consistent-giving-during-pandemic.html.

56 "Churches Divided on Web Use," Lifeway Research, January 21, 2011, https://lifewayresearch.com/2011/01/21/lifeway-research-finds-churches-divided-on-web-use/

57 "White Christians Have Become Less Motivated to Address Racial Injustice," September 15, 2020, https://www.barna.com/research/american-christians-race-problem/

58 https://www.npr.org/2020/07/17/891600067/multiracial-congregations-may-not-bridge-racial-divide

59 *Ibid.*

60 *Ibid.*

61 "What Americans Think About Women in Power," March 8, 2017, https://www.barna.com/research/americans-think-women-power/

62 CBE International, https://www.cbeinternational.org/content/cbes-mission

63 Price, Paula Frances, "Are Some Complementarian Practices Gaslighting?" October 17, 2019, https://www.theartoftaleh.com/are-some-complementarian-practices-gaslighting/

64 West, Steven D., "Christian Ethics," 2020, https://www.thegospelcoalition.org/essay/christian-ethics/

65 Gilson, Tom, "Handling Ethical Issues: Five Reasons Your Church Probably Isn't Teaching Enough on It," July 21, 2018, https://stream.org/hot-ethical-issues-five-reasons-church-teaching/

66 West, Steven D., "Christian Ethics," The Gospel Coalition, https://www.thegospelcoalition.org/essay/christian-ethics/

67 "Pastors Prefer Lay-Led Initiatives to New Church Programs But Struggle to Develop Leaders," May 6, 2020, https://www.barna.com/research/inspire-people-to-action/

68 "10 Truths of Churches That Do a Great Job With Leadership Development (Part 2)," June 11, 2019, https://leadnet.org/10-truths-of-churches-that-do-a-great-job-with-leadership-development-part-2/

69 Olsen, Dr. Howard, OnStrategy, "Church Planning Part 2: Elements of Your Strategic Plan," https://onstrategyhq.com/resources/church-planning-part-2-elements-of-a-strategic-plan/

CPSIA information can be obtained
at www.ICGtesting.com
Printed in the USA
LVHW030358090223
739019LV00006B/220

9 781663 223630